T0129944

Cosmic Conflicts

Cosmic Conflicts

Freedom isn't free, The only chance, The blood and the covenant, The ultimate assignment

Jonathan Ezemeka

authorHOUSE®

AuthorHouse™
1663 Liberty Drive
Bloomington, IN 47403
www.authorhouse.com
Phone: 1-800-839-8640

First published by AuthorHouse   10/25/2011

ISBN: 978-1-4567-8127-9 (sc)
ISBN: 978-1-4567-8128-6 (ebk)

Printed in the United States of America

This book is printed on acid-free paper.

ACKNOWLEDGEMENTS

I am very grateful to God almighty who confirmed his word on me that He will use the foolish things of this world to confound the wise and the weak things to confound the mighty. It is based on this truth that I dedicate this book to all the missionaries and fellow believers serving the Lord in different capacities and in different places. I pray God will use this book to open their eyes to this simple truth that our enemy the devil is defeated and that he is fighting hard to keep us ignorant of this fact.

My special thanks goes to Rev. Amechi Nwachukwu of the Amazing grace Assemble Enugu Nigeria whose preaching on this topic Cosmic Conflicts helped inspire me to write these series. My special thanks also goes to my friends at St Cyprians Anglican church Abakpa Nike Enugu, Evangelical fellowship communion of Anglican church [EFAC] St Cyprian branch, Scripture Union Abakpa main group all in Enugu state Nigeria. I will not fail to mention people like Rev. Obi Ahaiwe , Mrs. Ngozi Enyiobi, Jacob Onyia, Sunday Nwokolo and many others. I am also grateful to Mrs. Winnerfaith Ibrahim the wife of the Nigeria trade commissioner here in Taiwan who helped to encourage me in this work. I am especially grateful to my late sister Mrs. Celina Eze and her prayers to God for my salvation and my cozen Mr. Frank Ezemeka who has been very close to me and has supported me throughout the period of writing this book . . . Our good Lord will reward you all accordingly.

My special thanks also goes to Marcus Van who wrote a summary of the book, Rev. Fari Rider who did the first editing and who encouraged me to go ahead and publish this work . I am personally grateful to Mrs. Jennifer Chau who in spite of her tight schedule helped me in different ways to correspond with my publisher. I use to see this vision only for Nigeria and Africa but since you all who are not part of my culture believe in it, I now see it as a global vision. Finally I will not fail to mention my late father Ogbuefi Simeon Ezemeka and his last words to me two weeks before his death in June 2010,; that whatsoever a man plans to do and puts his faith in God no matter the time it takes it must surely come to past.

FORWARD

Reading of this work is not for the weak hearted or the closed minded. The Author pulls no punches in portraying how evil forces work to influence, deceive, and to destroy lives. He does not gloss over the affects sin has in our lives. You must be willing to approach it from a spiritual point of view while understanding that the world we live in is harsh and the ruler of this world is cruel. This series relays this reality in a very real and descriptive way while at the same time showing the power of the blood of Jesus to defeat every plan of the enemy.

Growing up in small town America in the middle of "the Bible Belt," the first time I read Cosmic Conflict I was unprepared for the "in your face," uncensored, transparent portrayal of the Spiritual Warfare that truly exists in this present world. We often quote the Scripture, "For our struggle is not against flesh and blood, but against the rulers, against the authorities, against the powers of this dark world and against the spiritual forces of evil in the heavenly realms" (Ephesians 6:12 NIV) but how well do we actually comprehend the battle that is taking place every day and every minute in the Spiritual realm? And how often do we fight to help prevent the evil forces from gaining a foothold in our lives and in the lives of those we love?

Now having spent over 17 years ministering in a Country where evil forces are extremely overt and relentless, I am more aware of the desperation of our enemy and the authority the Body of Christ has been given to defeat every attack of the enemy.

For people who, like me, lived most of their lives unaware of the works of the enemy this will be an eye opening work. It will cause you to understand more and hopefully pray more.

For people who are presently under the attack of the enemy this series will offer you a very real hope and a way to break free.

I trust this work will at the very least challenge your thinking and the way you approach Spiritual Warfare.

Rev. Fari Lee Rider

Missionary

Cosmic Conflicts. Things Don't Just Happen, They Are Justly Caused.

Preface by Harry L. Leid, Senior Pastor Agape ICA, Taipei, Taiwan.

I have personally known the author of this book for six years. He has shown that he believes and lives everything he has written in this book. In our International Assembly he leads our prayer ministry, and prays from the depth of his experiences in his home country of Nigeria.

Bullshit, what has it got to do with my life? Can she offer me the freedom I need?.

Ok let's see this one,

[He picks another book and starts to read]

VOICE—Satan now confiscates the products that originally belonged to God, in the history of mankind, man needs to take responsibility for restoring the lost world and wealth to God. Therefore since this world's goods have been pilfered from God you can cheat and steal money from the descendants of Satan.

More bullshit, suppose I am caught stealing, what happens? I will be locked up for years.

[It is at this stage that his door bell rings and he goes and opens the door for his girl friend Becky, he held her and tried to kiss her but she refused, he did that several times but each time she said no. This time he left her and went and sat opposite her in silence]

BRIGHT

I can see you are no longer interested in our relationship, may be you have found a foreigner in that church and if I may ask why have you chosen to become a Christian. Your parents have never gone to church even one day, we all belong to the same culture and religion. Who is the guy, is he an American, a Canadian, black Africans or American blacks?

BECKY

[Very surprised]

FREEDOM ISN'T FREE

SCENE 1

Bright is a young man who has determined in his heart to seek for spiritual powers, in this particular moment he is seen going through some books dealing with occult science page by page

BRIGHT

[Soliloquizing]

I have attended many teachings on esoteric science and belong to so many clubs and secret societies but none could bring peace of mind. In each I seem to be more in bondage.

Don't do this and don't do that.

[He picks up another book]

Let me see this one and what are they saying—:

VOICE—The infinite mother the immortal mother, old lady, who lives in the vast, limitless heaven which cannot be seen by human eyes

1

He is a strong believer in combating the forces of darkness with the power and blood of the Lord Jesus Christ. His Anglican background in Africa gives him a strong base to write this book. He likes to attack the forces of evil working in someone's life with fervent prayer. He also likes to emerge victorious in prayer over the forces of darkness.

The interwoven changes of scenes in this book well reminds us that all of us are engaged with outside of this life forces that attack and try to destroy believers in the Lord Jesus Christ. The book is a constant reminder that we are in spiritual warfare twenty-four hours a day. The only ones who do not recognize this are the sleeping Christians.

The marvelous truth of the Gospel is seen in the fact that we know who wrote the last chapter of history for this planet. God is in control now and will be when the last chapter of history is written. The key to this book is the last sentence, "I SURRENDER ALL."

Pastor Harry Leid

Yes, I knew you would say that my parents are saying the same thing too but the truth remains that I was introduced to Christ by the Pastor's wife who happens to be my student in the language school. And I tell you the truth my encounter with Christ has given me a kind of freedom that is beyond human imagination, its like am a new born baby. Christianity is not a religion where people go about searching for God or making one for themselves. It is ones personal relationship with a living God who came in the form of a man searching for his own people. Why not give Christ a chance into your life, you are always telling me you are still seeking for the truth, Christ is the way, the truth and the life. He has filled my emptiness and can do the same for you. Stop exposing yourself to Satan by seeking for wisdom where it does not exist. Occultism has nothing good to offer except misery, fear and confusion. I know you've visited so many temples in India, China, Tibet and in so many other places you have not told me about but if I may ask to what advantage and what positive changes did it bring to your life? The bible says that people keep searching for knowledge without coming to the truth.

BRIGHT

[Looking very angry]

So you think you can come here and insult me on what I believe. There is nothing in Christianity that can change my life. According to occult science Christianity is a lazy man's religion. How can you convince me that the death of one man can deliver us from sin? Your Jesus died for his own sin against the Roman empire. It is only a person with brain damage will put his faith in that.

[He gets up and opens the door for her]

I can see you're calling our relationship quits.

BECKY

If you want me to go I will but I have this to tell you, it is you that Satan wants to brain wash, atheism is a cannibalization of man's intellect. I still love you as a person but the spirit that rules your life is contrary to Christ who rules in me. I will continue to pray for you may be one day your eyes will be opened to behold the truth.

[She closes the door and leaves]

BRIGHT

[He sat down alone and started to reflect on his past]

FLASH BACK

Bright dressed in a kung fu uniform, practicing a step with his spiritual teacher. Next, sits with his teacher near a burning fire, drinking hot tea.

BRIGHT

[Looking directly at him]

Master if I may ask what is absolute truth?

[They look at each other for a long time]

TEACHER

What do you mean?

BRIGHT

Almost all religion claims to be leading mankind into the truth, what then is the absolute truth.

TEACHER

My boy you've a very curious mind, I know you're destined for something great, just be patient and you'll come to fulfill it. My work now is to guide you into exposing your inner potentials for the benefit of mankind.

[Looks at him in a very serious manner]

To me that stands as the absolute truth. Any truth that does not benefit mankind is not absolute.

BRIGHT

He came to his senses when his cell phone rings he picks it up, listens, then answers

Ok I will be in the club right away

SCENE 2

Bright is seen in a night club with some friends. He plays poker for some time before going to the gambling machine but he won nothing. Next he is seen in the drug section where he smokes some pot and finally he buys some drinks and sits in a corner sipping his drink. As he drinks his wine his mind went back to his encounter with Becky.

FLACH BACK

[With special effect his encounter with Becky was relayed to him.]

BECKY'S VOICE—Jesus Christ is the way, the truth and the life.

He becomes fully alert when a pretty lady walks into the club towards him. She sat a few tables from his. They look at each other while she made sexy appeals to him. Bright becomes fully interested and smiles back at her. Next she gets up and starts to dance in a provocative manner to the soft music from the live band.

Bright just sits there sipping his drink smoking and watching her at the same time.

This time she dances in front of him and bids him to join her, which he did.

After they danced for a few minutes, she opens her bag, brings out a white handkerchief, wipes her face and does the same to Bright.

LADY

[She stops dancing and starts to move outside while dragging Bright along]

[She looks at him with a smile]

Now follow me

[Bright follows her like a zombie outside into the darkness. She goes straight into a grave yard and stands before a gate that looks like a palace. She stops at the gate and made some incantations, the gate opens and they walk in. They go through a passage made of gold and stop at a door with the number

666, she knocks at the door three times and the door opens. Inside the room Bright becomes shocked when he sees the beauty of this room. The bed is made of gold with two golden statues dressed like ancient Roman soldiers, standing at the two edges of the bed].

Please just feel at home.

[She opens another door and a man dressed in suit walks in and smiles at Bright]

TERRITORIAL SPIRIT

[Very serious]

Bright we have monitored you for a very long time and we are impressed with your zeal to know the truth. You have a very curious mind and a burning desire to know the truth. You are chosen for a special mission on earth. You are welcome.

BRIGHT

[Confusion written all over his face]

But who are you and why am I here?

TERRITORIAL SPIRIT

She will explain everything to you.

[With that statement he closes the door and leaves

LADY SPIRIT

[She looks at him with a seductive smile]

Follow me

She takes him to the end of the passage and opens a door to what looks like a hall. Inside this hall he sees many evil spirits of different shapes and sizes in chains.

Immediately the door opens, they all shout freedom three times and stop.

The lady spirit blows a whistle and they shout freedom three times again and stop.

She then turns to Bright]

You are chosen to give them freedom to explore the world. They have all waited for this moment.

BRIGHT
What do you mean?

LADY SPIRIT
Just wait and you'll see.

[This time she locks the door and starts going back to the former room]

Come let's go

When they reach her bedroom she undresses herself in front of Bright and before Bright could recollect himself she pushes him to the bed and starts to seduce him. But she only uses these tactics to chain his two hands and legs to the bed. Afterwards she gets up, dresses herself and leaves the room.

The moment she leaves the room the two statues move like robots towards the bed where Bright lays. Meanwhile an overhead lamp switches on automatically and the room becomes brightened like operating room. This time Bright seems to fall into a deep sleep. While one of the golden statues starts to operate on his head, the other statue supplies the materials.

SCENE 3

[Becky weeps in the presence of the Pastor and his wife].

PASTOR

Now Becky the shedding of tears will not solve your problems, I advise you to put your faith in God. Now what exactly did you see in your dream about Bright?.

BECKY

Pastor what I saw in my dream is really horrible, it is difficult to explain, deep within me I believe Bright is in a great danger.

FLACH BACK

[Becky is seen in her bed tossing from one end to another like one having a nightmare, suddenly she finds herself in a wedding hall where Bright is about to wed but to her surprise when Bright unveils the bride, behold she is a lady with the head of a cobra. Becky screams and wakes up.

PASTOR

[Nodding his head]

I see, if I may ask, are you still in love with him?

BECKY

[Still weeping and wiping her face]

The issue is not about our relationship anymore. The issue is that he is getting involved into something unreal and demonic. I feel so guilty because I failed to handle the situation right the last time we met. I believe this has pushed him into this terrible relationship, please Pastor we need to do something to save him from this marriage.

PASTOR'S WIFE

You are not yet sure he is getting married. Even if he is what can we do to stop him?

PASTOR

My wife is right. The only thing we can do now is to pray for God's intervention in his life. But before we do that, what exactly do you want God to do in his life?

BECKY

I think he is going the wrong way. I know him very well, he is open minded and very sincere in his search for the truth. I want God to reveal this truth to him and lead him to walk the path of righteousness.

PASTOR

That's ok. Let us pray.

SCENE 4

After what looks like surgery on Bright's head the two statues go back to their former position and the bright light goes off with an alarm. Immediately the lady and the Territorial spirit come in and unlock him and take him to the room they came from.

While inside this room the Territorial Spirit goes straight and sits on his executive seat, the lady sits in front of what looks like a giant computer.

TERRITORIAL SPIRIT

[Pointing to the only visitor's seat]

Bright you can now sit down

BRIGHT

What is going on here and what have you done in my head.

TERRITORIAL SPIRIT

[Looking at the lady who seems to be waiting for his instruction]

You can now activate.

LADY SPIRIT

[She starts to operate on the computer]

> COMPUTER SCREEN
> ACCESS GRANTED
> CHIP IMPLANTATION
> OK
> READY FOR INSTRUCTIONS

BRIGHT

[He seems to relax this time with a smile]

Now what do you want me to do?

TERRITORIAL SPIRIT
[Smiling and looking at the lady]

Now Mr. Bright you are the first man on earth to reach ultimate consciousness, no one has ever reached that state of perfection in the history of man. The divine creator the queen of heaven has sent men on earth throughout history to guide mankind into this state of consciousness but none has made it but, rather those sent became victims to their own mission, namely Buddha, Jesus, Mohammed, Gandhi, Moses, Carl Marx, Socrates and others. They tried to lead mankind into this state of consciousness but could not. You are to lead mankind to a state of perfection.

LADY SPIRIT
[She gets up from her seat]

During creation man was made in the form of a computer with specific software's needed to make him function properly under direct control and regulation by the creator.

[This time she goes back to the computer and starts to type on the keyboard]

Now look at this

COMPUTER SREEN
VOICE Gen. 2:17

Voice—And the Lord God commanded man of every tree of the garden thou mayest freely eat. But of the tree of knowledge of good and evil thou shall not eat of it for in the day that thou eatest thereof thou shall surely die

TERRITORIAL SPIRIT

The human central processing unit is limited to function effectively with certain software which will give the divine creator absolute and total control over mankind. By this the human race can only depend on him for their daily function. This symbolic tree of life represents these group of software's while the symbolic tree of knowledge of good and evil represents the group that separates the human race from the divine creator, thereby giving man ultimate control over his destiny. This symbolic tree is the power that moves the earth, it is the nature of divine existence but in man it can be easily manipulated by external body.

[To the lady]

Go on

[She continues to type on the keyboard]

COMPUTER SREEN

Gen.3:22—24

VOICE—And the lord god said, Behold, the man is become as one of us, to know good and evil: and now, lest he put forth his hand, and take also of the tree of life and live for ever. Therefore the Lord God sent him forth from the garden of Eden to till the ground from whence he was taken. So He drove out the man; and he placed at the east of the garden of Eden Cherubims, and

*flaming sword which turned everyway, to keep the way
of the tree of life.*

TERRITORIAL SPIRIT

It would have been a terrible mistake if these two symbolic
trees were allowed into man, therefore evil will reign forever.
The only way to have this symbolic tree of life is to do away
with the tree of good and evil. Your mission on earth is to
help the human race do away with this software, good and
evil, and guide them into a state of ultimate perfection on
their own ready for eternity. That is your mission.

SCENE 5

ONE YEAR LATER

*[Bright is seen here addressing about 20 new members in his
courtyard of his newly acquired imperial perfection institute.*

*In the background of this courtyard 2 groups of about 10 each
are also seen perfecting the spiritual exercise that will lead them
to perfection. In a special room members are going through a
special identification process before being granted access into
the hall. After waiting for a while Bright emerges with his
overall red garment]*

BRIGHT

Today marks a turning point in the struggle of mankind
to attain spiritual perfection. You are the first group in the
history of mankind to be fully qualified to receive power
from the divine creator. Therefore you are now to go into
the world and purge yourself of this burden called good and
evil. Good and evil are inseparable and are the products of
choice made by man the very day he was created. It requires

the same choice from man himself to do away with it. The price of this purge must be paid by some one else. Although certain group of people spread the falsehood that the death of a certain man on the cross has set them free from the forces of good and evil. That is a big lie every man is a master of his own destiny.

Now you take your position of silence for in silence and tranquility you show your strength.

[They all sit in silence with their legs crossed while Bright starts to make incantations and speaks in strange tongues, with the two statues standing behind him. With special effect the spirits of those sitting are seen leaving their bodies one after the other in ball like objects and entering the open mouth of one of the statues. At the same time out of the open mouth of the other status comes the same ball like form of objects entering the bodies of those sitting.

SCENE 6A

SPIRIT WORLD

With special effects the evil spirits in chains were seen breaking loose one after the other with a shout of FREEDOM! FREEDOM! FREEDOM! And at the same time the spirits of the members of the club were seen taking the place of these demons, two powerful demons were seen loosing their chains and transferring them to the members of the institute one after the other as they appear.

SCENE 6B

[An interview conducted among members of this group to show the success of his teaching, this include healings of different types and the testimony of peace of mind]

SCENE 7

A MONTH LATER

[Mr. Lee sits for dinner with his family, which is made up of the wife and two children, Jack and Cindy.

Mr. Lee sits in silence and rarely touches his food.

LEE'S WIFE

[Looks upset and keeps looking at the husband]

My dear what is wrong with you? You are not eating any more and for the past two months you seem to be a stranger in this house. What is wrong with you, what have I done wrong? Look at your children; they are very confused because you have lost your cheerful self. Tell me dear what is wrong?

MR. LEE

[Looks at the wife as if she is a stranger]

I need freedom! That's' what I need now or never.

[He gets up and starts to move towards his bed room upstairs while the wife and the kids stop their eating and watch him in silence. As he goes upstairs the daughter also follows behind but in secret. As he enters the room she stands and waits, by

this time tears start to roll down her chin. As she notices the door opening she runs into another room and hides herself but watches through an opening. She sees the father with a long knife coming out of the room moving downstairs. With special effects; the echo from his thought are been relayed.

VOICE ECHO

Do it now. Do not fear. Purge yourself of good and evil. Do it and be free. Man is a master of his own destiny. It is the only way to ultimate perfection.

DOWN STAIRS

[The wife is seen weeping while her son Jack tries to console her. She stops weeping as she notices her husband's presence behind them. She becomes frightened when she sees him with a knife. Immediately he stabs the son from behind and as the wife gets up to stop him she gets stabbed in the chest. The daughter who sees everything runs back into the room and locks the door. She starts to shout through the window and throws down objects while the father bangs on the door. Already a handful of people have gathered to watch outside the building. Mr. Lee uses a very big box to smash the door open and when she sees him inside with knife and blood all over his body she jumps through the window and smashes herself on the tarred road. Mr. Lee comes out to the balcony before a large crowd of people, his two hands making the victory sign and shouts

FREEDOM ! FREEDOM ! FREEDOM.

POLICE

By this time an ambulance and the police have arrived. One group takes the corpse of the daughter while a handful of policemen try to reach out for him upstairs. But before the police could reach him he jumps and smashes himself close to where the daughter landed.

SCENE 8

[The Chief of police and his field officers are having a round table discussion concerning the gruesome family massacre]

CHIEF OF POLICE

From the report we've got, Mr. Lee came from a descent family background with no record of violence. He used to be a good husband and a good father but one thing that caught my attention is that recently he enrolled and became a member of the Imperial Institute of Perfection.

MR. CHUNG

Going through our reports I have discovered that this marks the third person from this institute who has committed such gruesome murder. A university student went to his girlfriend's room murdered her and came out with hands full of blood shouting freedom. A woman last week drowned her 6 month old baby and came out shouting freedom and now Mr. Lee

MR CHOU

Wait a minute, you said they shouted freedom. That's exactly what an eye witness said Mr. Lee shouted before he committed suicide.

CHIEF OF POLICE

Now if I may ask what do we have against the institute

MR. CHOU

Not much, it is just a religious group that teaches freedom from evil and how to receive spiritual perfection from god or whatever. To me they sound good.

CHIEF OF POLICE

How about the leader of the institute do we have anything on him.

MR CHUNG

[Reading from a desktop computer]

Nothing very unusual, he was once member of many cults, student under the great guru Janji he spent small time on drugs used to night clubs suddenly came to open the institute claim to have received divine perfection claiming to be the first man to receive it.

CHIEF OF POLICE

Any girl?

MR CHUNG

[Still reading from a desktop computer]

Deeply in love with a girl named Becky

She claims to be born again

Found mostly in a church lead by an America missionary

And they seem not to be close anymore.

CHIEF OF POLICE

Ok gentlemen we must continue our investigation from all angle but for now the institute and the leader sounds clean to me. The three incidents might be coincidental

SCENE 9

BRIGHT

[Alone with anger written all over his face].

THOUGHTS ECHO

- *what kind of freedom is this*
- *I can't even sleep*
- *The police by now may be linking me with all these murder*
- *What is really going on*

[There is a tap on his door, the lady spirit comes in.

LADY SPIRIT

What is wrong with you, you are now famous, you've got the power and the money.

What else do you want? And you have me at any time.

BRIGHT

[Looking at her directly in the face]

I NEED FREEDOM!

LADY SPIRIT

[She laughs]

You who gives freedom to people now begs for freedom. Ok now

[She seems to be serious now]

Freedom for what?

BRIGHT

Freedom to be what I used to be and from what have you put me into.

Members of the institute have become the talk of the town, some are killing their children, wives, husbands, girl friends and so on.

The police might have by now put a tail on me. Please tell me, what is going on? This is not the freedom I preached to the people. I never told them to kill each other.

LADY SPIRIT

The whole thing might be coincidence, your followers are growing world wide, no one can charge you for a small percentage of crime committed by them.

Just think of the position you hold in the society, the money, the power, the connection and the women. Do you want to loose all of them?

BRIGHT

What use are they to me? I say what use are they when everything is taken away from me? What is the use, even my manhood is taken away from me. I can't have a family, you are the only woman that can arouse me. What's the use of all this and if I may ask who are you? And what do you want from me?

LADY SPIRIT

I will tell you something, freedom is never free. Let's look at it this way, a country fights for freedom and gets it, that's just the beginning of their problems a lady wants freedom from her parents and gets married , that's where her problem starts and so on. Ok I tell you what I want—

[She opens her bag brings out a white handkerchief and throws it on his face, he falls asleep on the chair.

She goes straight to her pc clicks it on and the territorial Spirit appears on the screen.

TERRITORIAL SPIRIT

Yes something is wrong somewhere

LADY SPIRIT

Our mind control chip seems not to be working properly. There is an external interruption.

TERRITORIAL SPIRIT

I have monitored the situation and now look

COMPUTER SCREEN

[Showing Becky, pastor and the wife praying]

Yes you must do something about it she wants her boy back

LADY SPIRIT

[Anger written all over her face]

No he is mine and no one takes him from me.

TERRITORIAL SPIRIT

Be careful because the situation is becoming complicated, we need to reprogram him again

SCENE 10

Becky is alone in her room. Her mind goes back to the good time she use to have with Bright. With special effect these good times with Bright are relayed, even the times she tries to preach the gospel to him.

THOUGHT ECHO

Look at you baby in two months time you'll be 30years old.

No boyfriend and no hope of getting married.

Who do you think will marry you in this church.

All your sisters are married and you are here waiting for God's time

Stop pretending every woman needs a man, believer or no believer, after all flesh is flesh. Look at your boyfriend Bright he still loves you and wants you back, why not give him call.

PLOT 11

[As Bright begins to recover from his short slumber, the lady who sat by the computer stops and watches him]

BRIGHT
[Looking at her in anger]

What have you done to me?

[His cell phone rings and he listens]

Hello oh my god Becky

Please I need you now.

You called at a very good time

Not here I will tell you later

Ok 5pm our usual

I still love you

LADY SPIRIT
[She looks at him with anger written all over her face]

Who is she?

Remember no other woman besides me

BRIGHT
[Gets up and starts to move towards the door]

You are crazy

[They look at each other for a very long time before Bright slams the door and leaves]

SCENE 12

Becky is seen here getting into her car and driving off at about 4.30 pm.

As she drives towards the road leading to the park a police patrol car intercepts her and asks her to stop.

She obeys, and turns off the engine. She was asked to shift to the passenger's side while one of the policeman took the steering, while the other took the back seat. They drove off leaving the police's car behind.

BRIGHT

At exactly 5pm Bright is at the park waiting for Becky, and one hour later he called her number but no answer. As he sat in that park his mind went to the good time he had with Becky even all the times she tries to convert him to Christianity. He looks at the time now, it is 7.30 pm and he calls the number again but this time it's the spirit lady's voice

LADY SPIRIT

Who are you and what do you want?

BRIGHT

[Looks shocked]

What have you done with her?

HELLO ! HELLO!

[This time the line went dead]

Bright sat down disgusted

SCENE 14

Two sisters Sarah and Emily were roller-skating along the private road leading to the park. About 200km from their starting point stood a police car.

SARAH

Now Emily lets see who can reach that police car first.

EMILY

Ok, let's go.

SARAH

[Sarah the senior who happens to be the first to touch the car notices an usual noise from the car trunk.]

Emily, there is a noise in that car's trunk.

[The noise was so loud that it attracted the attention of people passing by who later called the police. When the police arrived they forced the trunk open only to find two police officers in their underwear with their mouth taped.

SARAH

[Sara calls for her sister laughing at the same time]

Emily let go

SCENE 15

[A man drove Becky's car to a road leading to the mountain and stopped the car opposite the cemetery].

BECKY
[She looks out as the car stops at the cemetery gate and behold a man and a lady stood at the passengers side]

Who are you and why am I in this place.

LADY SPIRIT
You are warned for the last time, leave Bright alone he belongs to me.

[The lady opens her bag takes out a handkerchief and threw it on Becky's face]

BECKY
[She fainted and slumps into the car seat]

SCENE 16

THE POLICE STATION
[The two police officers are seen standing before the police chief]

POLICE CHIEF
What exactly are you telling me, that a man and a woman came to you and threw a handkerchief on your face, then what happened?

MR CHUNG
It was exactly how it happened.

MR CHOU

The lady opened her bag brought out the white handkerchief and threw it on him while the man touched me on the passengers side where I was sitting and when I turned to see who touched me, he did the same to me.

POLICE CHIEF

[Starts to laugh]

You mean I should put what you've just said in writing.

[Lowering his tone]

Ok how come two of you were naked in your car boot.

I suspect two of you paid a visit to the prostitutes without paying.

Why not tell the truth let me see how I can help you.

[The telephone rang and he left them to answer the call]

SCENE 17

AT THE CHURCH

[The pastor and the wife all seen having a discussion and they both looked worried]

PASTOR'S WIFE

The mother called and says she is not yet back.

PASTOR

And she is supposed to be here by now for the lady's meeting

PASTOR'S WIFE

The mother wanted to call the police but I asked her to give her more time.

PASTOR

[Making a call through his cell phone]

Ok let me try her cell phone again

Becky is it you,

What happened?

Accident?

Ok

Which hospital?

Ok we will be there

[Speaking to his wife]

Becky is in the hospital

PASTORS WIFE

What happened?

PASTOR

She did not give me the details, we must hurry to see her

SCENE18

[Bright is seen driving home at a top speed. Later he is seen rushing into his room and straight to the screen on the wall.

BRIGHT

[Looking at the Lady spirit who appeared on the screen full of smiles]

What have you done to her?

LADY SPIRIT

I can see you still love her.

BRIGHT

[full of anger]

I said where is she?

LADY SPIRIT

You need not to worry about her, she is fine. I just warned her to keep away, next time it might be terrible for her.

[At this time Bright s cell phone rings, he veils the screen and leaves to answer the call.]

BRIGHT

Oh my God

Becky are you Ok. Its alright I know about it. Where are you now.

Ok I will be there

SCENE 19

[Becky is seen lying on a hospital bed while the Pastor and his wife stood beside her, a nurse is also seen checking her pulse and temperature.

PASTOR
[Immediately the nurse left]

Becky what really happened?

BECKY
[In tears and with an effort manages to sit up]

Its difficult to explain, Pastor something terrible is going on in this city and Bright is at the center of it.

PASTOR'S WIFE
What happened?

BECKY
I called Bright and he sounded so terrified and he wanted me to meet him at the park. According to him he has something to tell me. So I prepared myself to meet him.

[With a special effect the clip from her encounter with the policemen to the time they left her at the graveyard was shown]

PASTOR

Who are they and why the cemetery?

BECKY

[Shedding tears]

I don't know Pastor, something terrible is going on.

[The nurse opens the door and Bright walks in]

BRIGHT

[Looks impatient and disorganized]

Please Becky you must leave this hospital now, it is no longer safe for you.

BECKY

[looking confused and frightened]

Why?

BRIGHT

[Trying to lift her up]

I will explain later, please let's leave, this place is not safe.

[Turning to the Pastor]

Do you have a safe place she can stay for a while?

PASTOR

Ok maybe we can use the church's quest house.

SCENE 20

[The pastor, his wife, Bright and Becky sit together in a serious discussion]

BRIGHT

[Looking frightened]

Becky you are right I have made a wreck of myself. My search for the truth has opened the door for some evil beings to invade this city.

BECKY

Please Bright what have you gotten yourself into and how? It's like our lives are in danger.

PASTOR'S WIFE

It's time you open up and stop carrying the load alone. We have been praying for you.

PASTOR

And you said the hospital is not safe for Becky, why?

BRIGHT

Ok I will start from the beginning

[looking at Becky]

On the day I had an argument with you , I left and went to the club

[With special effect the clip from the time to his encounter with the lady spirit and the territorial spirit is relayed].

When I started this Imperial Perfection Club [IPC], I really thought I had found the answer to what I was looking for. I was teaching them physical and spiritual techniques that would help them to be free from earthly problems and worries. The testimonies were poring in and people loved my teachings. The turning point came when some members became involved in terrible crimes. Some were killing their kids, wives and friends for freedom. I never taught them that, something is wrong somewhere and only these two evil couples can explain that well. That's the reason I want you out of the picture while I strengthen things.

PASTOR

This is terrible indeed. How Bright, if I may ask, do you think you can face them, knowing fully well you are dealing with spirits? The bible says in Eph. 6:12 that we are not fighting against flesh and blood but against spirits. Hiding yourself from them will not solve your problem because by now they might know you are here with us.

From now on I believe we are targets to their attacks but that does not bother me now, its you. You need to lean on a higher spirit more powerful than theirs and Jesus Christ is your only hope.

BRIGHT

I will if your Jesus proves himself to me

PASTOR

That's Ok, would you mind if I pray for you

[Bright nods his head]

Ok let us pray.

SCENE 21

The pastor lays on his bed, turning from one end to another like one having a nightmare or a dream.

He saw Bright under the weight of a dragon, next he came closer and starts to rebuke the beast in the name of Jesus Christ and immediately as the beast comes to attack him he wakes up. He kneels down and starts to pray.

After prayer he picks up his phone and dials Bright s home number.

TERRITORIAL SPIRIT

Yes, who is speaking?

PASTOR

I am pastor James, can I speak with Bright

TERRITORIAL SPIRIT

There is no one with that name here

[He hangs the phone]

PASTOR

[He dials the number again but no response]

SCENE 22

[Bright wakes up and finds himself in a dungeon with chains on his legs, he tries to survey the new environment but the chains on his leg can not let him move further.

BRIGHT

[Soliloquizing]

Oh my God what exactly is the meaning of all this.

God? Which God indeed? Do I really believe in the existence of God at all?

Becky, Pastor and his wife, all believe but how can there be a God when these evil spirits control everything.

I wish they were in my shoes right now, so we could tell who the real God is.

After some time he drifted into a sleep.

SCENE 23

[The pastor, his wife and Becky were seen knocking and at the same time pressing the door bell to Bright s house. After a long wait, the door opens from within and standing before them is a lady and a man.

When Becky saw them she screamed and fainted.

Immediately the Pastor and his wife tried in vain to revive her, later he called the ambulance services and the police. Within

20 minutes the ambulance and the police arrived at the scene. Later the Pastor and his wife were seen reciting the whole incident to the police

POLICE

And where is the lady and the man.

PASTOR

When she slumped they just went in and locked the door in our face.

POLICE

[Pressed the door bell several times without response]

Are you sure some one is in there?

PASTOR

Yes, we saw them.

POLICE

[This time the policeman turns the key lock and the door opens and they go in only to see Bright sitting and smoking with ease.

BRIGHT

[Upon seeing the policemen he got up to welcome them]

POLICE

Why didn't you answer the door bell?

BRIGHT

Oh I was too busy and besides I thought you were a sale's men.

PASTOR

Bright, are you Ok? Where are the people with you, a lady and a man? They were the ones that opened the door for us just now.

BRIGHT

A Lady and a man! What are you talking about? I am alone.

POLICE

You mean there is no one here with you? Ok come on outside with us.

[While outside the ambulance attendance have already put Becky on a stretcher and they were about taking her into the van]

Your girl friend saw these two people and fainted, so who are they and why are you hiding them.

BRIGHT

I really don't know what you are talking about.

PASTOR

Officer I believe something is wrong here. I am very sure we saw these two people.

BRIGHT

Pastor there is nothing wrong with me rather it is you and your God that is very wrong.

[Turning to the police]

Officers you are free to search everywhere for them if you will]

[As the police went in to search the rooms, the ambulance leaves the premises with it's siren on]. The pastor and his wife stand speechless watching Bright

BRIGHT
[Looking at them]

You can join them and see for yourself.

[He left them and went into another room]

PASTOR'S WIFE
[They looked at each other with shock]

Are you sure this is Bright? He does not show any feelings at all, even when he saw Becky lying helpless on the stretcher.

PASTOR
Let us leave this place something is wrong here.

SCENE 24

POLICE CHIEF
[Reading from a report while the two police officers stood at attention in front of him, after a while he gently drops the piece of papers on the table and starts to speak to them directly.]

I believe this case is somehow linked to your run in with a man and a lady

.[He laughs]

I am not so sure, therefore I am handing over to you two this case.

[He gave them the report]

I want you to do a thorough investigation on the pastor, the wife, the church, the girl Becky and the boyfriend Bright. I believe this will help root out the cause of the high rate of crime in this city and expose those behind it all.

POLICE OFFICERS

Ok sir

SCENE 25

Becky is still on the hospital bed but fully awakes with an IV still running in her veins, standing beside her is the doctor and the two police officers.

DOCTOR

[Speaking to Becky]

Becky I believe you can speak to them for just a few minutes?

Can you do that?

BECKY

[Nods her head]

Yes!

DOCTOR

Ok, gentlemen please just for a few minutes, she is still recovering from the shock and she is weak.

[Exit doc.]

1ST POLICE MAN

[He asks the question while the 2nd police man writes]

Becky from our report you had an encounter with this couple before.

BECKY

Yes!

1ST POLICE MAN

And that one of them threw the handkerchief on your face.

BECKY

Yes!

[This time the two police officers look at each other]

1ST POLICE MAN

Ok Becky , I think we are through with you for now. Thanks.

[Exit police men]

1ST POLICE MAN

We must speak to her boyfriend they might be the same group of people we encountered.

SCENE 26

[Few minutes later the Pastor and his wife walk in]

PASTOR'S WIFE

Becky how are you? I can see you are getting better.

PASTOR

Becky what really happened? Do you know those people?

BECKY

[She sits up at this time]

They are the two evil spirits that took me to the cemetery.

PASTOR

I thought as much.

PASTOR'S WIFE

Can you believe, that when we entered the house with the police officers they were no where to be found in the whole house?

BECKY

What do you mean?

PASTOR

Yes! We could only see Bright and he looked odd to us.

PASTOR'S WIFE

He looked at us as if we are total strangers and even when he saw you unconscious on a stretcher he never reacted at all. I believe something is wrong here.

BECKY

[Looks frightened]

What do you mean that he acts odd

PASTOR

Becky I want to read some passages from the bible, maybe the Holy spirit may use them to explain the situation more—:

> *VOICE—Mat. 16:23 But he turned, and said unto Peter, Get thee behind me Satan: thou art an offense unto me: for thou savourest not the things that be of God, but those that be of men.*

Yes even Christ looked at Peter and knew it is no longer Peter speaking but Satan and He addressed him directly. Paul finally summarizes this in his letter to the church in Ephesus—:

> *VOICE Eph. 6:12 For we wrestle not against flesh and blood, but against principalities, against powers, against the rulers of the darkness of this world, against spiritual wickedness in high places.*

From now on you should be careful whenever you are with him. We will continue to pray for him. Let us pray.

[They joined hands together in prayer]

SCENE 27

[The two police officers are now at Bright s house knocking and pressing the door bell at the same time]

VOICE

Come in the door is open

POLICE OFFICERS

[They open the door and walk in, only to behold a man and a woman dancing cha—cha—cha.

1ST POLICE OFFICER

[Speaks in whisper]

Are you sure they are not the man and the woman?

2ND POLICE OFFICER

Maybe not, these ones look younger.

THE COUPLE

[They continue their dancing without paying any attention to the visitors].

1ST POLICE OFFICER

[With harsh tone]

Where is Bright!

THE COUPLE

[This time they dip their hands into their pockets and bring out white handkerchiefs and start to wave them while they dance towards them.

POLICE OFFICERS

[The two men look at each other and run out of the room]

2ND POLICE OFFICER

Why did you run out from them?

1st POLICE OFFICER

Are you blind? Didn't you see the handkerchief?

2ND POLICE OFFICER

[Looks frightened]

You mean they are the same people? Lets leave here.

[They go straight to their car and drive off]

1ST POLICE OFFICER

[While inside the car]

Now what do we do? It is a stupid idea to run away from them. They may not be the same people.

2ND POLICE OFFICER

Suppose they are, this time they may keep us totally naked and the boss will accuse us of going to visit prostitute again.

1ST POLICE OFFICER

So what do we do now? If we fail to crack this case the same boss will continue to believe we visited the prostitutes and refused to pay them. I think we should go to the temple or we should consult a spiritualist for solution.

2ND POLICE OFFICER

Let's go back to the hospital again and speak to the girlfriend. I strongly believe that Bright and this strange couple hold the key to this mystery.

1ST POLICE OFFICER

I am really confused.

SCENE 28

[Becky is reading a bible when a nurse walks in]

NURSE

There is a young man who wants to see you

BECKY

Who is he?

NURSE

A man named Bright

BECKY

Let him in

BRIGHT

[Walks in]

Becky how are you?

BECKY

I am fine Bright why did it take you such a long time to come to see me?

BRIGHT

[He is interrupted by the entrance of the two police officers]

1ST POLICE OFFICER

Bright you are the one we are looking for.

2ND POLICE OFFICER

We were in your house some few hours ago and found a man and a woman dancing, who are they?

1ST POLICE OFFICER

And what are they doing in your house?

BRIGHT

You should have asked them if you really saw them in my house and beside I don't know them.

1ST POLICE OFFICER

We saw them in your house and I believe they were the same group of people your girl friend had an encounter with and fainted. These two people are a mystery and you know something about them.

BRIGHT

What do you mean by a mystery?

2ND POLICE OFFICER

The mystery is in their handkerchief so if I may ask who are they?

BRIGHT

Are you sure you can defend what you are saying in a court of law

2^(ND) POLICE OFFICER

That's why it's a mystery. Who are they?

BECKY

Bright you mean you don't know those people?

BRIGHT

I ran a big organization, with many people, how can I know all of them?

BECKY

But these two people were in your home not your office. They opened the door when pastor, his wife and I rang your door bell. Bright who are they?

BRIGHT

Until I see them myself for now I can not say who they are.

SCENE 29

[With special effect the pastor and his wife were seen entering the premises of the hospital while at the same time the 1^(st) police officer is seen talking to Bright.

1^(ST) POLICE OFFICER

You will join us at the station to clarify some issues.

BRIGHT

Are you going to arrest me or what?

2^(ND) POLICE OFFICER

You are going to help us in our investigation.

PASTOR & WIFE

[Walk in and both were shocked to see Bright].

PASTOR

[With special effect as the pastor looked at Bright s face he was able to see in a flash of the moment the face of the lady and that of the man reflected in Bright s face. The pastor looks at him and speaks with a strong voice—:]

I command you now in the name of Jesus Christ who are you?

[Bright starts to gyrate like a serpent and wants to attack the pastor but he stood his ground and starts to speak in tongues, commanding the evil spirit to come out of him in the name of Jesus Christ.]

BRIGHT

[He falls on the floor while the pastor and wife were praying over him even Becky joined them to pray. With special effect the Lady and the man were seen leaving the body of Bright while he lay motionless.

DOCTOR

[Walks in with a nurse]

Who are they? And why are they running away?

1ST POLICE OFFICER

Which people Doc.?

DOCTOR

We saw a man and a lady leaving this room in a hurry.

1ST POLICE OFFICER

[Speaking to his partner]

Let's go after them, they are the people we are looking for.

[To the doc.]

Which direction did they go?

DOCTOR

Towards the car park

SCENE 30

SPIRIT WORLD

[Bright sits in pain and agony with chains on both hands and legs inside the dungeon, when suddenly there is a great light followed by a voice which echoes—]

VOICE—: I am the way, the truth and the life.
[The chains on his hands and legs broke to pieces]

SCENE 31

[The two police men run out into the parking lot, quite a number of people were seen in the park. They stand and survey the whole place and suddenly they see a man and a woman about to enter a car. Already they have started to attract a lot of attention because of the guns in their hands].

THE MAN & THE WOMAN
[Shock written all over their faces as the two police men point their guns at them]

POLICE OFFICERS
[They put their guns back because the two people look older but when the woman opened her bag and brings out a white tissue to wipe her sweating face the 2nd police man runs away from her.

1ST POLICE MAN
[Starts to laugh when he sees what happened]

THE MAN
Please officers what is all this about?

1ST POLICE MAN
We are really sorry sir it's a mistaken identity.

[He goes straight to his partner. They both sit at a sidewalk and start to laugh]

2ND POLICE MAN
I hope this case will not send us into a mental home.

1ST POLICE MAN
Please lets get out of this place.

[They go straight to their car still laughing]

SCENE 32

[As the pastor and the wife continue to pray over him in tongue the doctor and the nurses were battling to revive him also. With special effect the body of Bright is seen entering his lifeless body on the floor].

BRIGHT
[He gets up and sneezes twice]

PASTOR'S WIFE
Glory be to God. Bright are you Ok?

BRIGHT
[For the first time he reacts upon seeing Becky on the hospital bed]

Becky why are you here? And me?

[He looks around]

What's going on here?

[Even the doctors and nurses are all surprise]

PASTOR
What really happened? Are you Ok?

SCENE 33

As they were still laughing and about to start the police car, the lady and the man who hid on the back seat of their car throw the handkerchief on them, they drag the driver to the back seat, while the lady takes over and they drive off.

SCENE 34

BRIGHT

[This time he goes to Becky and sits near her].

Becky what really happened? And why are you here?

BECKY

I am fine it's you I worry about. What's going on in your life?

You are acting so strange to us.

BRIGHT

I know! It's like a dream, I was in a pit, no! it's like a dungeon with chains on both my hands and legs.

PASTOR

So what happened?

BRIGHT

Suddenly there was a great noise and a voice echoed

I am the way the truth and the life and the chains broke to pieces.

[Turning to Becky]

I remember you saying that to me several times.

PASTOR

[Picking up his bible and opening it]

Bright I want to read something to you but before I do that I want you to listen to me. You have received a direct word from God and it's a rare privilege.

[He gives the bible to him]

Now read John 14:6

BRIGHT

[Taking the bible from him he starts to read]

"Jesus said unto him, I am the way, the truth and the life, no man cometh unto the father but by me".

Oh my God this is actually written in the bible, I thought it was just a joke.

PASTOR

Now Bright Christ has set you free from these demons, are you now ready to invite him into your life and make him lord over you?

BRIGHT

[Kneeling down]

I am ready to die for him.

PASTOR

[Laying his hands on him and starting to pray]

SCENE 35

POLICE CHIEF

[Sits in discussion with a couple]

You mean my men pointed guns at you for what if I may ask?

THE MAN

I can't understand, it's the most awful situation I have ever faced in my life.

THE WOMAN

And they were acting very strange.

POLICE CHIEF

So after that what happened?

THE MAN

They just went to the side walk and started laughing over it.

POLICE CHIEF

Wait a minute! Are you sure of what you are saying?

THE MAN

I am too old to make a joke out of this. My wife here is a living witness she was so shocked she vomited in the car. It is not a joke, please call these men to order before they cause great harm to people.

POLICE CHIEF

Pleas be assured I am taking this information very serious.
I am really very sorry for the sad experience you had with
my men.

[They shook hands and left]

SCENE 36

PASTOR

How do you feel now?

BRIGHT

[Looks happy]

For the first time in my life I can feel real peace in my
mind.

*[At this stage the two police officers walk in with guns in their
hands pointing at Bright]*

1ST POLICE MAN

You are under arrest and any thing you say now can be used
against you in the court of law.

DOCTOR

[Tries to stop them]

But he is still my patient

BECKY

[Starts to cry and tries to stop them]

2ND POLICE MAN

He is wanted for all the killings going on in this city. So let go.

[They put handcuffs on him]

BRIGHT

Becky it's ok. I have got the freedom I wanted throughout my life.

I am ready for whatever.

[They took him in their car and drove off]

SCENE 37

[The two police officers found themselves in a dungeon with hands and feet bound with chains.]

1ST POLICE MAN

[Tries to survey the environment]

How did we end up here

2ND POLICE MAN

I told you this case would cause us to wind up in a mental home.

1ST POLICE MAN

I would prefer a mental home over this place.

SCENE 38

[They drove the car outside the hospital gate with great speed and right in front of them a truck is trying to overtake another truck. In order to avoid a head on collision the police driver swerved to the right sending the car into a ditch. The car windshield breaks to pieces, the two police officers come out through the car windows and managed to force Bright out through the same window. Before the arrival of the ambulance and police the two police officers have already ordered a man out of his car under gun point, push Bright inside and drove off.

SCENE 39

[The accident scene has attracted a lot of people including the doctor the, nurses, the pastor and his wife even Becky managed to be there. The police chief has also arrived with his men and every one wants to speak to him. The man whose car was taken, the doctor, the nurses, the pastor even Becky wants to speak to him

POLICE CHIEF

[Speaking at top of his voice]

Please I want to hear from one person at a time.

[To the doctor]

Now doctor what happened? You were the one who called me.

DOCTOR

Your men walked into my hospital and arrested a patient under my care which is against the law without showing any arrest warrant

THE TRUCK DRIVER

And they caused this by their reckless driving.

[Pointing at his car and the police car]

THE MAN

At gun point they ordered me out of my car and drove off with it against my wish.

THE POLICE CHIEF

[Speaking through his cell phone]

What is your license number?

[To the man]

THE MAN

Blue Nissan Tiena FW433

THE POLICE CHIEF

Alert all area patrol command to arrest and detain two police officers or any occupant in a blue Nissan Teana with registration number FW 433. For your information the officers are armed and could be dangerous.

[Turning to the crowd]

Now gentlemen and ladies be assured the situation is under control

[To his men] let's go

SCENE 40

BRIGHT

[Fear written all over his face]

Where are you taking me? You're going too fast.

1ST POLICE OFFICER

[Pointing his gun at his face]

Keep quiet or I'll blow your head off.

2ND POLICE OFFICER

Our men on patrol, what do we do now?

1ST POLICE OFFICER

We will tell them we are on duty. I am sure an alert for our arrest has not been sent.

2nd POLICE OFFICER

[At a little distance ahead stand two police officers beside a police patrol car while another police officer sits at the wheel]

How can you be sure?

1ST POLICE OFFICER

It's a gamble.

[At this time they come closer to the patrol team]

1ST PATROL OFFICER

[Walks closer towards the Nissan car and smiling as he noticed the 2ND police officer at the wheel]

Mr. Chou What's going on? You are suppose to be on patrol today.

1ST POLICE OFFICER

[Sitting with Bright at the rear]

Our patrol car got ditched while we were on duty, we are using this as an emergency vehicle

BRIGHT

[At this stage Bright managed to open the car door and threw himself on the ground, shouting.]

They are not on duty they kidnapped me from the hospital.

PATROL OFFICERS

[The patrol officers held him while the 1st police officer comes out of the car and tries to drag him back into the car. It was at this stage that the patrol officer's walkie-talkie starts to receive message for the arrest of the occupants of the blue Nissan.]

1ST POLICE OFFICER

[When he heard this he ran back into the car.]

Move fast, they have just received the alert message to arrest us—MOVE!

2ND POLICE OFFICER

I can't see again

1ST POLICE OFFICER

What do you mean can't see? I said move fast, they have just received a message for our arrest.

[Starts to rub his eyes]

Wait a minute I can't see either.

2ND POLICE OFFICER

Are you deaf? I can't see I am blind.

[They heard the sound of gun shots and their four tires were deflated and immediately a voice was heard]

1ST PATROL OFFICER

Come out of the car with your hands up. If you make any suspicious moves we have been ordered to shoot.

POLICE OFFICERS

[They come out with their hands up moving like blind men.]

SCENE 41

POLICE CHIEF

[In discussion with the Pastor, Pastor's wife and Becky]

I can see clearly from this report,

[Putting the report on the table], submitted by my men who are now on the run that there is a mysterious couple involved in this case.

[Turning to Becky]

You had an encounter with them and you Pastor and your wife claimed to have seen them. If I may ask who are they and where are they now.

BECKY

To be frank sir these two people still remain a mystery to me and my encounter with them started with your men but later ended up with them.

POLICE CHIEF

What do you mean?

BECKY

I have to start from the beginning

[Once again the video clip starting from her encounter with the police officers to the time she was left at the tomb is relayed]

POLICE CHIEF

This is really terrible and now Pastor do you have anything to say about this.

PASTOR

Sir before I say anything to you I have to read a portion of the bible to you first.

POLICE CHIEF

What has the bible got to do with this? The media is making a wreck of the police organization and the leaders are on my neck. Already my two officers are widely reported to have gone crazy

[Throwing the newspapers on the table]

Some claim my men are involved in kidnap while others claim they are raping women, the report about us is terrible. I need information to get to the root of this case and not to listen to your gospel.

PASTOR'S WIFE

Sir from what Becky has just told us and from the report your officers submitted you can agree with us that the issue at stake now is more spiritual than physical. I strongly believe that for you to get to the root of this matter you need to change tactics from your traditional way of crime detection to some thing else.

POLICE CHIEF

Like what madam? Dancing! Singing! Praying and reading the bible!

While the whole city is about to explode! Why! Because two crazy police officers are loose on the street.

I am not a Christian and do not believe in your bible!

PASTOR

[Becoming impatient and bold]

Chief I want you to listen and listen very well, things don't just happen they are caused to happen. Now if I may ask you can you explain why [1] a teenage boy should walk into his class pull out a gun and begins to shoot both his teachers and fellow students [2] a man walks into his own house rapes his daughter and shoot her dead or why a crown prince took a gun and shot every member of the royal family at a dinner and even why a man should pull out his gun on a crowded street and begins to kill Chief, can you explain that. Have you asked yourself why all the death penalties and harsh punishment could not reduce crime in any given society.

POLICE CHIEF

[*With two hands wide open*]

To be frank for my 28 years of active service I have found no reason why people should commit such crimes or why any one should destroy his own family or even kill others for the fun of it.

PASTOR

Now I will tell you something

[*To Becky*]

Open your Chinese bible and give it to him to read from 2nd Corinthian 4:18

BECKY

[*Opens her bag, takes a bible, turns to the verse and gives it to the police chief*]

POLICE CHIEF

[Took the bible from Becky and starts to read]

> *Voice—2ⁿᵈ Corinthian 4:18 While we look not on things that are seen, but at things which are not seen: for the things which are seen are temporal: but the things which are not seen are eternal.*

[He looks at the pastor]

So what has this got to do with the issue at stake?

PASTOR

This is the root of most of the crimes in the world today not just this city. The man and the woman you are talking about may not be real and your two officers in their present condition may not be real also.

POLICE CHIEF

[Looks surprise]

What are you trying to insinuate that the couples are spirit while my officers have become ghost or what?

PASTOR

I will answer that with another passage in the bible, now lets read Mark 5:2—3

BECKY

[Takes the bible from him opens to the verse and gives it back to him]

POLICE CHIEF

Voice—Mark 5: 2—3 And when he was come out of the ship, immediately there met him out of the tombs a man with an unclean spirit. Who had his dwelling among the tombs; and no man could bind him; no, not with chains.

[*He drops the bible and looks at Becky*]

I remember you said something about these couples taking you to the cemetery

[*Looking at the Pastor*]

You mean they are spirits

PASTOR

That is exactly what I think and that your officers have already been possessed by these spirits.

[*At this stage the telephone rings and he picks it up*]

SCENE 43

[*The ambulance and the police cars have just arrived in the hospital, Bright and the two police officers lay on different stretchers each and are taken into the emergency with heavy police escort. The nurses and other paramedical staffs are seen putting the necessary equipment in place. The two police officers who seem to be unconscious are put in a ward while Bright is kept in a room opposite. The doctors at this time have started doing some preliminary test on them already.*]

DOCTOR
[*Looking at Bright with a smile*]

Bright I think you are fine apart from these little scratches on your face

[*Touching his face*]

BRIGHT
It was when I fell out of the car. Its ok I am fine.

[*At this stage the hospital premises witness the arrival of the police chief and his entourage which include the pastor, pastor's wife and Becky. The doctor after shaking hands with them led them first to see Bright who is being guarded by two police officers.*

BECKY
[*She ran ahead of them to hug Bright, kissing him and at the same time touching the scratches on his face.*

Are you Ok

DOCTOR
He is fine and is free to go unless you still need to talk with him.

[*Looking at the police chief*]

POLICE CHIEF
We may need him later for questioning but not now. Where are my men Doc?

DOCTOR

[Leaving the pastor, his wife and Becky behind he led the police Chief into another room opposite which is also been guarded by two police officers.

POLICE CHIEF

[He went straight to the officers who lay unconscious with IVs running through their veins on the bed and inspected them one after the other, after which he starts to speak to the 1ˢᵗ patrol officer on duty]

What happened did you have a fight with them?

1ˢᵗ PATROL OFFICER

Not at all sir, I stopped the Nissan car just for a routine check

FLASH BACK

[With special effect the video clip from the time the patrol officers stopped them to the time the two came out with their hands up walking like blind men was shown]

POLICE CHIEF

But why are they lying here unconscious?

1ˢᵗ PATROL OFFICER

I just can't tell sir. When I saw they had complied with my instructions I then told my assistance to go ahead and handcuff them but before he could reach them they both fell down unconscious.

POLICE CHIEF

And so,

1ST PATROL OFFICER

I had to call for an ambulance and additional help

[At this stage the pastor walks in with his wife, Becky and Bright]

PASTOR

{*When he looked at the two unconscious men on the bed their faces reflected in a moment that of the man and the lady]*

[Turning to the police chief]

Would you mind if I pray for them?

POLICE CHIEF

That's ok, do you want us to leave

PASTOR

Not at all! You can stay there is nothing secret about it.

[As he looks at them again the reflection came again and this time he raised his two hands covering both of them :—

Father in the name of Jesus Christ I take authority according to your word in Mark16:17

> *Voice—And these signs shall fallow them that believe, in my name shall they cast out devils and they shall speak with new tongues.*

Therefore in the name of Jesus Christ and by the authority in His name I command you unclean spirits to come out of them now.

[Immediately the two men start to shake violently and making awful noise]

1ST POLICE OFFICER
[Speaks with a female voice]

This body belongs to me and no one can send me out

2ND POLICE OFFICER
[Speaks with a male's voice]

This city and its people belongs to us, my people needs more bodies to be free

[This time the pastor, his wife and Becky start to pray in tongues while the two men continue to gyrate violently like wounded snakes.

PASTOR
[Lays hands on both of them]

I command you unclean spirits to come out of them in the name of Jesus.

[With special effect the man and the lady were seen leaving the bodies of the two officers and immediately the two men calmed down and start to focus their attention on people around them.

THE TWO POLICES
[Rubbing their eyes]

I can see again

SCENE 44

POLICE CHIEF
[*Surprised and Confused*]

Mr. Lee and Chou, what is wrong with both of you?. Are you ok?

PASTOR
Chief I believe now the evil spirits have left them, you can see they are back to normal. They are free.

POLICE CHIEF
I see! Now both of you, do you have anything to say about all this?

1ST POLICE OFFICER
[*Still rubbing his eyes*]

The last I can remember is:—

FLASH BACK

With special effect the video clip from the time they were laughing inside the car and the time the lady and the man pounced on them from the back seat of the car was shown until the time they were in the dungeon.

PASTOR
So after that do you still remember anything else?

2ND POLICE OFFICER

After some time we noticed the dungeon shaking as if there was an earthquake and suddenly

FLASH BACK

[*With special effect the two police officers were seen in the dungeon with chains on both hands and legs and suddenly the whole place starts to shake with a bright light and a great noise*]

Voice—I am the way, the truth and the life

PASTOR

Sir I will want you to read another verse in the bible

[*To Becky*]

John 14:6

[*Becky opens the bible verse and gives it to him*]

POLICE CHIEF

[*Takes it from her and starts to read*]

Voice—Jesus said unto him I am the way, the truth and the life no man cometh unto the father but by me.

This is really terrible, the exact words spoken to them in the dungeon is the same in your bible.

You may not convince me to become a Christian but this particular case has taught me a great lesson I will not forget.

For the past 28years I have served the government, I now believe the govt. and its law enforcement agents have wasted a lot of money and man power in persecuting, condemning and putting in jail innocent people while the real criminals are free.

THE END

JONATHAN EZEMEKA
DADICATED TO MISSIONARIES SERVING THE LORD IN DIFFIRENT PARTS OF THE WORLD

The Only Chance

SCENE 1

ALONG THE MAJOR STREET IN ENUGU

At the major street in Enugu the members of the New life church evangelism group are seen distributing tracts and at the same time preaching the gospel to any one who cares to listen. Within the group is another group of people in a low bed trailer, mounted with an open address system. At the background of the music a voice is hared inviting people to a power pact crusade.

At a very short distance from this scene Chief Ogbuefi Akulue Uno is in his Mercedes V boot giving instruction to his driver to stop and move at intervals while at the same time he looks left and right the street looking for some one.

At a point he seems to have seen what he is looking for when he orders his driver to stop.

Chief Ogbuefi

[*In a very strong voice*]

Nkech!

Nkechi

[*Her father's voice shook her and she leaves the people she is preaching to and goes to him*]

Oh daddy?

Chief Ogbuefi—

[*Opens his car and comes out, anger written all over his face*].

Where is your mother?

Nkechi

[Points at her across the road talking to a group of people]

[*This time the mother who seems to have noticed the presence of her husband leaves the people she is talking to and starts to come towards him*].

Chief Ogbuefi

[*With a very angry voice*] go and call her!

[*This time Sister Mary comes in Chief looks at her with anger*]

Both of you get inside the car.

[*Nkechi the daughter wants to say something but because of his angry look shuts her mouth. As soon as they are in the car Chief orders the driver to move*]. [*While inside the car chief looks at his wife with great contempt*]

Ogbuefi Chief

Mary you are a disgrace to my family and my person in this society. First look at the way you are dressed, the wife of Chief Ogbuefi Akulue Uno has joined a group of hungry looking people roaming the street like beggars.

Sister Mary

Dear what is wrong in been a Christian? Why this public embarrassment.

Chief Ogbuefi

[*Interrupting*]

Don't dear me! For the past few days you've totally abandoned the house and today I want this issue settled once and for all. Each time I come home for launch you're out for one program or another.

[*As he continues to pour out his anger the wife just sits down quietly. This time the car enters their compound and stops. Chief goes straight into his room and brings out their marriage certificate, removes his wedding ring from his hand and places these items on the table*]

Chief Ogbuefi

Now bring out that ring.

[*The hesitates*]

I say bring out the ring before I get angry with you.

[*She brings it out and gives it to him*].

Now listen to me. I am now giving you this chance till 7 o' clock tomorrow morning to make a choice between Jesus and I who is your husband?

Sister Mary
[Very shocked and surprised as tears roll down her chin]

Dear what do you mean?

[Moving closer towards him]

Dear are you quarreling with God? What is really going on in your life now? Previously you were not disturbed about my going to fellowship but now I think something is wrong. Oh my God.

[She just breaks down and starts to weep]

Chief Ogbuefi
[Ignoring her and turning to his daughter]

For you when I've finished with your mother I will also give you your own condition.

[After saying this he leaves them and goes straight into his secret room].

SCENE 2

AT THE UNIVERSITY HOSTEL
Johnny wakes with a start as a result of unusual noise from his room mate, Ebube who sleeps at the next bed. Ebube is visibly shaken and grasping for air. He sweats allover his body. Johnny

*throws away his sheet and runs to him as he struggles with invisible hands of death. Johnny is confused; he tries all sorts of things including rubbing wet towels allover his body. At a stage he stops and goes into serious praye***r.**

Johnny

Father in the name of Jesus I take authority over every plans of the enemy to take away this life. I pray down the fire from above to destroy every gathering or manipulation of Satan and his agents against Johnny.

[He continues to pray with authority while Ebube lies on the floor still breathing heavily]

Ebube

They want to kill me They want to kill me.

SCENE 3

THE ULTIMATE CLUB ANNUAL GENERAL MEETING.

The hall is decorated in a mystic form with candles, burning incense, a shrine and the wall painted with all kinds of satanic artistic work. A casket sits at the center with a big mirror covered with red lining standing in front of the casket. Members of the group numbering around 6 are seen walking calmly around the casket.

Each of the members holds a shinning sword with exception of Chief Ogbuefi. Behind the shrine sits a priest while his ape like creature who serves as errand boy stands between the shrine and the other members. This time all seems to be calm.

The Chief Priest
[*With a voice full of horror*]

Chief Ogbuefi Akulue Uno

[*He moves towards the ape like creature and stands*] *The creature goes up to the shrine and takes a long sword and gives it to him]*

What is article 666 of our club secret code.

Chief Ogbuefi
That I Chief Ogbuefi Akulue Uno will be willing at any given time to make any sacrifice required of me by the club without question.

Chief Priest
And you forget to mention the fact that the club reserves the right to take any action if you fail to comply. Meanwhile my record shows that you joined this club as a bachelor and that you have made a substantial contribution to the club in terms of money. May I now remind you that after today's sacrifice no man on earth will ever stand before you. The circle of 6 is for men with courage. Now you may proceed for the final ritual.

[*At this stage Chief Ogbuefi moves towards the casket]*

Now unveil the mirror.

[*He does so*]

Now strike the image.

Chief Ogbuefi

[*Shocked when he sees the full image of his son glaring at him.*]

No! No! No! I can't! my only son?

Chief Priest

It is too late my son you have no alternative

[*At this stage his closest friend Chief Odobra comes closer to him and starts to speak into his ears.*

Chief Odobra

Ogbuefi please just strike the mirror and every thing will end. Your life here is in danger No person will allow you leave this place alive, now you've known the secrete.

[*Chief Ogbuefi just looks at him with contempt*]

Remember I am the one who recommended you, please do it, your wife is still a young woman she can still give you another son.

Chief Ogbuefi

[*Looking at him straight in the face*]-

I will rather die here than do it.

It is at this stage a thunderous noise is heard throwing every person into confusion. Smoke fills every place. Members are seen running for their lives. With special effect Johnny and his friends are also seen in serious prayers while this destruction is going on.

SCENE 4

UNIVERSITYHOSTEL
Two other student believers later join Johnny and help bring Ebube out from the bed on the floor while they join hand around him in prayer. This time he is already sitting while they continue in prayer.

SCENE 5

OGBUEFI'S HOME DRIVE
He is seen driving home in a top speed.

SCENE 6

CHIEF OGBUEFI'S COMPOUND
His security man is awakened by the horn blast. He gets up and peeps through the pinhole on seeing his master's car he immediately runs and opens the gate for him. Chief drives into his compound with the same speed.

SCENE 7

CHIEF'S HOUSE
The wife and his two daughters are awakened by the noise each of them emerging from their different rooms into the sitting room very confused.

Sister Mary
[Opening the main door]

Who might that be?

PLOT 8

CHIEF'S COMPOUND

Chief Ogbuefi opens the car door this time he becomes fully aware that he is still wearing the club's uniform made of animal skin. He is reluctant to come out of the car but it is too late because his wife and two daughters are already surprise in seeing him almost half-naked wearing an animal skin.

Sister Mary

My dear what is this you are wearing? And where on earth are you coming from in this rag and in the middle of the night?

Chief Ogbuefi

[*Moving past them like a zombie*]

Did you hear any news from Ebube my son?

[*With that statement he goes straight into his secret room. The wife wants to join him but the girls stops her.*]

Nkechi

[*Holds the mother*]

No mummy! Remember he warned us for no reason should any one enter that room.

Sister Mary

[*Sits down and starts to weep*]

Oh my God What has my only son got to do with all this? Your father is up to something strange. I know it. I also feel it. Oh my God.

[Raising her hand towards heaven].

Please heavenly father intervene and put a stop to this business.

[At this stage the telephone rings, Juliet runs and picks up the phone she listens for some time]

Juliet

Mummy!

[She shouts]

It is Ebube's room mate he says his name is Johnny.

[This time Chief comes out and takes the phone from her]

Chief Ogbuefi

Hello Yes I am the father do you mean he is still alive.

[He removes the phone from his ear and speaks to his wife and children]

Oh my God I thank you.

[He listens again and speaks]

Don't worry I will send my driver to pick you up.

[*He drops the phone and goes straight to his wife and holds her. He is really acting very strange*].

My dear Ebby is still alive.

Sister Mary

Dear what is really going on? tell me I am really confused.

[*They hold each other while the girls look at each others and go into their room*].

SCENE 9

AT THE ULTIMATE CLUB

At this stage the smoke is dying down gradually. The main hall is totally empty and in disarray. The chief priest and two other members of the club are seen panting in a small room that looks like a shrine. They all look frightened.

Chief Odobra

[*Looking at the high priest*]

What really happened?

Chief Priest

[*Looking more confused*]

How do I know. Let me consult our errand spirit first.

[He starts to beat a big drum and in each beating he makes incantations. With special effect system the errand spirit is seen on the screen in front of them.] We really want to know who

attacked us during the ceremony and from where this great force came from.

Errand Spirit

We are still investigating the source of that power please do every thing you can to speedy up that sacrifice. The gods are very angry, our top secret is exposed. I need not tell you what that means to your lives. The gods are really angry.

[Gradually the spirit fades away]. [The members just look at each other dumbfounded.

Chief Okura

Where do we start from here? Even the gods have no answer to our question.

Chief Odor

I know Chief Ogbuefi very well if he says no, then nothing can make him change his mind.

Chief Priest

He is your friend you know him better than us tell him he has no alternative. We are now facing a devil's alternative. Something must be done or else

[He just waves his head]

SCENE 10

AT OGBUEFI'S COMPOUND

Johnny and two of his friends are seen escorting Ebube out of the car. They lead him into the sitting room where the mother and his two sisters hover around him with tears of joy.

Johnny

[Picking his words carefully]

It was at midnight around 1.30am. I woke up only to notice Ebube struggling with an invisible hand of death. He was almost been choked to death by unseen attackers. I ran to him and helped him up. He was panting and struggling at a point of death. I did all I could but there was no way to save him until these brethren of mine came in and joined me in prayer. This morning thanks to God he seems to be okay.

[Raising his voice a little higher]

Chief I really don't know exactly what is going on in your family but one thing I can tell you is that your son is facing a high level spiritual manipulation from the highest order. There is a cosmic conflict going on in the world today, some school of thought call it the battle between good and evil, positive and negative, God and Satan or Christ and Satan as the case may be.

[Speaking now with great authority]

Satan is the brain behind all this. The bible says he has three missions on earth, to steal, to kill and to destroy. Now chief I want you to know this truth God almighty revealed himself in Jesus Christ in order to destroy every work of the devil.

[Speaking more directly to chief now.

The only solution to what is happening in your family now is Jesus Christ. This is your chance and the only chance.

[*Chief just looks at him with great surprise and confusion written on his face*].

Chief Ogbuefi

Thank you for your effort towards my son and thank you also for the good advice

[*giving him money*]

Take this for your transport back to school. As for what you've just told me I will think about it

[*The wife and the two daughters escort them out, as they are about to reach the door the doorbell rings as Juliet runs past them to open the door for Chief Odobra. He greets them casually and goes straight past them into Ogbuefi's secret room. Ogbuefi himself gets up and goes with him into the room.*

SCENE 11

CHIEF OGBUEFI'S SECRET ROOM

Chief Odobra

[*Goes straight to the point*]

Ogbuefi why did you do that? Didn't you say you desperately want to become a member of the inner circle?

Ogbuefi

YES! Did I bargain the murder of my only son as a condition for my entry?

Chief Odobra

And that a prayer house you attended prophesied that the only way you can get protection of life and your business is to join us. Did you or did you not say that?

Chief Ogbuefi

Yes I did but does that mean I should murder my only son whom then am I seeking protection for.

[Looking at him straight in the face]

If my son dies what is the need for the protection? I am now asking you Mr. Do Good. I have helped you in so many ways if this is your method of paying me back then you are a very wicked friend. I never joined the club for money.

[This time almost speaking to himself].

I thought the club could protect my family and me but I can see now that my greatest enemy is the club and you.

Chief Odobra

This issue you are toying with has gone beyond sentiments. It is an issue of life and death. It has to do with your life, my life, our families in general, including every member of the club. It is now out of our control. The only way to prevent genocide is your cooperation.

[He gets up]

If you still have something upstairs

[Pointing at his head]

Think fast and act this is your only chance.

Chief Ogbuefi

[*Gets up with great anger*]

Have you finished?

[*Pointing at the door*]

Now get out of my house!

[*They look at each other for a very long time then Chief Odobra leaves the room full of anger*].

SCENE 12

IN OGBUEFI'S SITTING ROOM

Sister Mary with her two daughters are sitting round Ebube who is lying on the sofa looking very tied.

Sister Mary

[*With tears*]

Oh my God what is going on in this house.

[*Turning to her son*]

Eby what is really going on? Have you joined the secret cult in the campus?

Ebube

Mummy you people should leave me alone I want to rest.

Sister Mary

I know it. Meetings, clubs, board this and board that. My spirit keeps telling me something sinister is going on and your father's behavior for the past few days is really suspicious. He hates the gospel, which is the most painful aspect of it all. Somebody who hates God, where does his help come from? Oh my God.

[She starts to weep]

[This time Chief Odobra comes out looks at them without saying anything and then walks out of the house].

[Chief Ogbuefi comes out also full of anger. He goes straight to a chair and sits down.

Juliet

[Standing up boldly]

Daddy, Mummy and even you Ebuka what the hell is going on in this house.

Ebube—

[Pointing at her]

Don't mention my name.

Sister Mary

[Gets up and sits near to the husband, she also places her hand on his shoulder and looks at him]

My dear what is really going on? Are you in any form of trouble? Remember marriage has made us one flesh. Your pain is my pain. Why do you want to bear the whole thing alone? Each time I looked at your face I always see a man battling with forces too great for him. My dear without Christ you can do nothing.

Chief Ogbuefi

[*Looking very weak and tired*]

The issue at stake has nothing to do with any of you. The little you know about it the better for us all.

[*Now sitting up*]

I want every one of you to listen and be calm. Our lives and especially that of Ebube are in great danger. I know the people I am dealing with. I will make every arrangement to send Ebube outside the country within the shortest possible time.

[*He gets up*]

Just trust me.

[*The whole family look confused. There is tension, even Ebube who seems unconcerned gets up and looks at the father. Chief just stares at them*].

I want you all to be calm about this, the situation is under control.

[*At this stage the two daughters run and hold him*].

Nkechi

Daddy what is happening, are you in trouble?

Juliet

Why is Ebube been taken out of the country at this time?

[*He just looks at them at a time they can not bear it any more. They all start to weep*].

SCENE 13

SPIRIT WORLD

In what looks like under water spirit effects, the territorial spirit responsible for the whole area summons all her field agents to an emergency meeting. In this gathering there are awful noises all over the hall.

First Spirit Agent

[*Whispering to another spirit agent*]

What is going on? Why this emergency calls?

Second Spirit Agent

How do I know. I was in the church when I receive the signal to attend this meeting.

[*At this stage there is a great noise as the territorial spirit is ushers in. Two lion faced evil spirits lead her into the hall. The moment she enters the hall all of the spirits rise from their seats and bow before her three times. Each one is accompanied with a great noise.*

Territorial Spirit
[*She looks really terrible with bulging eyes and very big breast*].

Who amongst you is responsible for the ULTIMATE CLUB?

[*One errand spirit stands up*] *Now where is my sacrifice?*

Errand Spirit
[*Trembling with fears*]

The final meeting to collect the blood was in progress when a force greater than ours descended on us and disrupted everything. My spirit agent has traced this force to a group of student believers praying for the victim as at the time of our meeting.

Territorial Spirit
[*Interrupting*]

I know about that! their prayers will always interrupt for a moment but what have you done about it?

SILENCE
[*She orders her two lion faced spirits to devour him. They bounce on him and tour him to pieces. There is dead silence in the hall. She leaves her position and goes round each member one after the other sniffing at them like a dog. She comes to one of them and stops, looks at her then sniffs at her again*]

You smell very awful and where do you serve?

Agent

Night club

Territorial Spirit

[*Laughing in an evil manner*]

Oh I know it you smelly HIV

[*They all burst into an awful laugh as she goes back to her position. Back in her position she automatically stops laughing and there is calm everywhere again.*].

I will handle the Ultimate club affairs myself. Now I want every one of you evil thing to listen. The issue at stake now is that we are advancing towards the final battle. Our target at this point in time is to make it impossible for the spirit of the righteous one dwelling in any human body to manifest itself. More than 2000 years ago we eliminated him physically on this planet and now he has carried the battle into the spirit realm. I on behalf of the prince of this world send you all into the world to fish out any human or group still harboring his spirit in them. Force his spirit out of that body, money, sex and power are at your disposal. He should not be allowed to pollute our human race. NEVER AND NEVER.

[*She bangs her fist at the table and leaves with the same noise she came in with.*]

SCENE14

AT THE AIRPORT DEPARTURE HALL

Chief is seen boarding the flight to Lagos, as he is about settling down in his seat a beautiful lady comes in and takes the seat next to him. Chief fastens his belt, looks at her and smiles. The lady smiles back also. She then tries to fasten her belt but can not. She is still battling with it when Chief undid his own belt and leans on her to help her fasten hers. They look at each other

Chief Ogbuefi

[*With a smile*]

I am Chief Ogbuefi Akulue Uno 1 The M.D and chief executive A.K Inter Biz Nig. LTD. And may I call you?

Lady B

[*With a smile full of seduction*]

I am Lady Beatrice working with the America embassy in Lagos. Just call me Lady B.

Chief Ogbuefi—Oh my God what a lucky coincidence that is exactly where I am going. I know these crazy Americans will not hesitate in giving employment to a piece of beauty like you. Where do you live in Lagos? I hope you live alone?

Lady B—I live with my parents.

Chief Ogbuefi—Oh I was expecting an invitation from you

[*still looking at her directly in the face*]

Lady B—How will I explain you to my parents.

Chief Ogbuefi

[*Almost biting her ears*]

Will you be able to explain to them if I buy you a drink in my hotel.

Lady B

[*Looking at him in a very romantic way*]

Is that an invitation?

Chief Ogbuefi—That is it

[*At this stage the plane lands and taxies to the terminal. They all disembark and go through the customs. Outside the airport lobby chief orders an airport taxi to take them to Ikeja airport hotel*

SCENE 15

AIRPORT HOTEL
At the hotel they both go to the reception where he books a double suit for both of them. The waiters escort them to their

room where chief makes orders for drinks and food to be served in their room.

Chief Ogbuefi—You see God has a way of making things work for me. You work with the America Embassy and I came to Lagos to process my son's papers for visa to U.S.A. What a coincidence. You see what I mean?

Lady B—Yes! I can see what you mean but Chief Ogbuefi do you really believe in God?

Chief Ogbuefi

[*looks at her sharply*]

Yes I do why do you ask?

Lady B—Why then do you want your son who may be graduating next semester out of the country now?

Chief Ogbuefi

[*More surprised now*]

How do you know about my son's schooling?

Lady B—

[*With an evil smile*]

News fly about.

Chief Ogbuefi—

[Alert and suspicious now]

Wait a minute I really don't even know much about you. Who are you?

Lady B—Do you really want to know me? Okay I will show you who I am.

[Within a twinkling of an eye she transforms herself and becomes the terrible territorial spirit.]

Chief Ogbuefi Akulue Uno I want you to listen if you fail to sacrifice that boy to me as you've sworn to do. I will destroy you and your family.

[Before she can finish her speech chief falls down and faints, it is the waiter who comes in and alerts the hotel security while Lady B is no where to be found. The security officer of the hotel makes arrangement for the hotel ambulance service to convey him to a nearby hospital.

PLOT 16

CHIEF'S HOUSE
Chief's personal secretary is seen working on the P.C when his telephone rings she picks up the receiver and listens for a moment.

Personal Secretary—Oh my God

[she shouts]

What happened? Ok wait a moment.

[She picks a pen with a shaky hand and writes something down while still holding the phone receiver to her ears. Later she drops the phone and rushes to the office of the general manager Mr. Obi Eke.

General Manager—

[Looks very shocked]

What do you mean? What happened?

Personal Secretary—The lady who phoned told me he checked in with a lady. According to her it was a waiter who saw him unconscious in their hotel room.

General Manager—What happened to the lady?

Personal Secretary—No where to be found.

General Manager—Yes I knew it, women will ruin him one of these days. He cannot resist anything in skirt.

Personal Secretary—What do we do now?

General Manager—We close the office for business today. Telephone his wife; book the afternoon flight for me to Lagos.

[As she turns to leave.]

Wait a minute make the necessary contact with his wife before you make the booking ascertain from her if she will be going with me please tell her nothing about the lady.

Personal Secretary—yes sir!

SCENE 17

CHIEF OGBUEFI'S SITTING ROOM
Nkechi is reading the bible while Juliet her junior sister is dressed in a sexy outfit singing the latest pop song

Nkechi—

[*Marks the page, closes the bible and looks at her sister.*]

Where do you think you're going in that outfit? It seems you're not concerned with what is going in this house. A person whose house is under fire is chasing the rat.

Juliet—

[*Looks at her with a crooked smile*]

And then what about it, am I the one who caused the fire? It is you and you're born twice attitude that is causing the whole problem. Look Baby I am going to have a good time with some guys.

Nkechi—Juliet the moment you come to your senses and begin to allow the word of God to have an entrance into your life.

Juliet

[*Interrupting*]

Hold your preaching we know what is going on in that your fellowship meetings. Okay?

[*Coming near to her*]

Look Baby everything in this world is cult system. You understand? You are in your own cult and I am in my own cult. Okay? Believer babes for believer's guys. The same for pirate babes who go for pirate guys. Bankers for banker's even doctors go for doctors.

[*She now bends down as if trying to bite her ears.*]

Local babes go for local guys. When you trespass that is when you become a sinner.

[*This time she stands up in front of her*

Forget it baby flesh is flesh after all I saw the way you were looking at Johnny Ebuka's room mate the last time they brought Ebuka back.

[*With eyes wild open and looking at her directly in the eyes.*]

How am I sure you've not gone to his room to pray together? Well I hope to join you people one of these days because I have seen cool, calculated, sexy and romantic guys in that your group.

[*She just walks across the room shaking her hips from side to side*]

<u>Nkech</u>i—May God almighty forgive you.

Juliet

[*Turning back to face her*]

That reminds me. Bob Dee your former boy friend desperately wants to speak to you.

Nkechi—Just tell him I am married to Jesus Christ.

Juliet

[*With eyes wide open*]

Will your Christ accept a non-virgin like you?

[*At this stage the telephone rings*]

Okay my virgin sister this call I believe is from my sweet heart calling for our regular jam together.

[*She demonstrates the current dancing step before going to pick the phone. She listens for a moment, her face changed as she shouts*]

Holy Moses Oh my God what happened?

[*She removes the phone from her ears*]

Mummy! Mummy!

[*At this stage the mother who was cooking in the kitchen comes out, Nkechi stands up while Ebube who is in his room comes out also.*]

That daddy is admitted in a Lagos hospital.

<u>All</u>—what!

Sister Mary

[*Goes straight and takes the phone from her in a shaky hand*]

Hello

[*She listens for a moment*]

Please book a seat for me. I will go with you

. [*She drops the phone and turns to Nkechi*]

Go and tell our president and prayer secretary what is going on.

[*At this stage tears starts to roll down her face. She turns and goes into her room to prepare when Nkechi comes in.*

<u>Nkech</u>i—Mummy

[*She turns with tears all over her face*]

Let us commit the whole thing first into the hand of God. No situation is too big for him.

[*She turns and looks at her daughter and tears have already started rolling down her face. They look at each other for some time before ending their prayers in warm tearful embrace.*

SCENE 18

AT THE HOSPITAL

Chief is being taken from the ambulance. The doctor is giving instructions to the nurses and other staff. They are rushing with oxygen equipment. The doctor and the nurses are putting the patient to a bed. It is at this stage that the spirit of chief Ogbuefi is seen with a special effect system leaving the body. Next he is escorted by two angels into the spirit world one at each side. They take him to a place where he was able to see the glory of the Lord and he is overwhelmed by its beauty.

Chief Ogbuefi—Oh my God what a beautiful place to be very splendid.

[One of the angels raises his sword and this vision disappears from him. This time they take him to another place as the same angel raises his sword again. What he saw shocked him. He sees the chilling agony of death, hell and people groaning in pains under sever burning heat. He looks back and sees that the two angels have left him in the hands of two terrible looking demons that have already started to push him forward. He kneels down and starts to weep like a baby]

Oh my God I don't want to be there just give me another chance.

[As he continues to weep and resisting them a thunderous sound is heard. The whole place becomes engulfed with smoke. When the noise died down, chief is left alone while the two demons disappear. He looks up only to see Jesus Christ appearing as in the same form during his ascension into heaven, blocking the entrance into the hell fire but this time he is standing on a pool

of blood. As he stands with his spread hands a voice is heard reading from the book of Mathew—26:28 FOR THIS IS MY BLOOD OF THE NEW TESTAMENT, WHICH IS SHED FOR MANY FOR THE REMISSION OF SINS.

This was followed by heavenly song

> *Oh I died for you shaded all my blood to set you free and to give you external life. Oh my son I have taken all your pains. Oh I died for you shaded all my blood to set you free and to give you another chance. Oh my son I have taken all your pains.*

SCENE 19

AT THE HOSPITAL
Chief's wife and his manager are seen discussing with a nurse on duty.

Nurse—you are the wife?

Sister Mary—yes. [*The nurse beckons to another nurse walking through the passage.*]

Please take them to the patient from the hotel.

The nurse leads them through a passage to a private room. She asks them to wait while she knocks at the door. The door opens and she goes in. After an interval she opens the door and asks them to come in. Chief is lying on the bed, breathing through an instrument. The doctor is writing some prescriptions on his folder. The wife starts to weep silently as she confronts the doctor.

Sister Mary—Doc. is there any hope for him?

Doctor—[*He just looks at her casually*]

Be calm madam. We are doing our best

[*turning to the nurse*] telephone Dr. Ogbonna and Dr, Philip the heart specialist to come up. Then you prepare the theatre for tonight

[*turning to chief's wife again*]

Madam we will do our best to help your husband. Okay?

[*With that statement he leaves the room*]

Sister Mary—[*Raises her hand to heaven*]

Oh my God have mercy upon him please father give him another chance. [*She weeps silently*]

SCENE 20A

CHIEF OGBUEFI'S HOUSE
At midnight there is a car with four men parked in front of chief's house. Three of them come out of the car wearing masks. Two of them hide while one knocks at the small pedestrian gate to attract the attention of the security man. As the security man opens the pedestrian door to ascertain their mission first before giving them access into the compound. He comes face to face with a man pointing a gun at him. With the help of the other two men hidden behind the pedestrian door they held him at a gunpoint after releasing a warning shot that froze him. The

three men start to beat him up and tie him to a chair. After this encounter they station one man at the gate with instruction to shoot. At any suspicious movement. They break into the main building crossing the sitting room, moving from one room to another. The leader alone goes into Ebuka's room and raises him from sleep and uses a white cloth soaked in chloroform to cover his face. He then drags him into the sitting room.

SCENE 20B

CHIEF OGBUEFI'S COMPOUND

The other two go into the girl's room and start tearing their clothes in an attempt to rape them. It is at this stage their leader comes in and releases another warning shot into the air.

<u>Gang Leader</u>—Stop it

[The two boys froze while the girls fall down and faint].

This is not our mission here. Let them go.

[The girls are left on the bed almost naked]

Now listen! Lie down and remain calm, if you make any noise we will come back.

[Turning to his men]

Let's go.

[Outside they dump Ebuka into their car and drive off.

SCENE 21

ESCAPE

They drive for a very long time and each time Ebuka sits between two gang members who give his unconscious body support at the back seat. After some time they slow down as they connect an unuttered road leading to a very big building that looks like a warehouse. As the car stops inside this compound the leader comes out and calls his boys together.

Gang Leader—I am going to meet our client just be at alert. Any suspicious movements shoot and explain later. Okay?

[They all nod their heads. He leaves them and goes further into the dark to meet a man in black suit carrying a black portfolio. When he comes to the man in black he then speaks aloud]

Bring the item*!*

[They bring Ebuka out of the car. This time Ebuka is starting to gain consciousness but still walks through the support of the gang men.

Gang Leader—Mission accomplished.

The man in black—

[Giving him the portfolios]

This is your money. Now I want you all to disappear.

[The leader takes the portfolios from him and goes into the car with his group and they drive off.]

SCENE 22

AT THE HIGHWAY

The gang is driving at a top speed. After an intersection their head lamb reveal a police security post away. As they come closer the warning light from the police post indicates that they should stop.

Gang Leader—What is going on?

Driver—The cops! What do I do now?

Gang Leader—It is too late now. Just watch out. It might be an ordinary routine check. Hide your guns. We tell them we are from the party.

At this stage the driver reaches the checkpoint.

Police Leader—*[Going round the car, flashing his touch light into their faces]*

O/C come and see—this na four dangerous looking guys oh. My friend where are you people going on this speed?

[At this stage two more police officers come down from the van to join him.

Gang Leader—O/C we are from the party.

Police Officer—Okay all of you get out.

Driver—[*In a very low tone*]

What do I do?

Gang Leader—Move back

[*The police officer seems to catch the joke, raises his gun and ready to shoot. It is at this moment he gets a shot from the gang leader. The car has already started to race backwards but one of the two policemen standing by shot and killed the driver instantly. The car runs into the side drain and stops. The police puncture the four tires and order them out with their hands up. One after the other they are all rounded up and handcuffed while the dead bodies of the police officer and the gang driver are all bundled into the police van and they drive off.*]

SCENE 23

CHIEF'S HOUSE
The two girls get up, managed to cover themselves up and are shaking like leaves. The shout of agony from the gate man frightens them more. The gate man's constant cries made them to sit up and start to tip toe from their room to the sitting room. At the sitting room the cat jumping from the seat make them jump and shout. They tip toed into Ebuka's room but the room is empty.

Juliet Nke where is Ebuka? He is not in his room.

[*At this stage the two start to weep but the gate man's constant cries bring them to their senses.*

Nkechi—It is Aboki the gate man. Lets go and see what 's wrong with him.

Juliet—Are you sure they're not there with him.

[*They tiptoe out moving like frightened rabbits. The gate man continued to shout for help. They go straight to the gate only to see the gate man tied to a chair with bruises all over his body. They run to him and start to untie him.*]

Aboki—Make una use knife under the bed.

[*Which they did.*]

Nkechi—Aboki where is Ebube? He is not in his room.

Aboki—They carry am comot

[*The two girls start to weep openly*]

Please make una no cry may be they want money from oga. Come make we go inside call the police.

[*They are still crying while he leads them inside*]

SCENE 24

POLICE STATION

The desk sergeant is seen sitting on his desk making some entries on materials submitted by a suspect before putting him into the custody. The police station is as usual busy with many waiting to be attended to. There is an unusual noise outside and people are seen giving way to an incoming group. Three young men are led into the station in handcuffs. People are rushing outside to see one of them lying in pool of his blood. The leader of the patrol team goes straight to the desk Sergeant.

Patrol Leader—O/C register these suspects for robbery. The following items were found on them, five loaded pistols, two A/K 47-assault rifles and 2500000 naira. We stooped them on the highway during our routine check, suddenly as the saying goes 'the guilty are afraid'. These boys opened fire on us killing one of my men. The desk sergeant and other policemen shouted in shock.

[*It is at this moment the telephone rings*].

Desk Sergeant—

[*Picking the phone*]

. Hello? Central police station.

[*He listens for a moment then hands over the phone to the patrol leader*].

I think this is from your area of operation.

[*The patrol leader takes the phone from him and listens for a while*]

Ok we will be there in a moment.

[*Turning to the desk sergeant*].

Robbery case at Chief Ogbuefi's house!

The desk sergeant gives him papers to sign, which he does and leaves with his men. Outside he disperses a group of people surrounding the corpse trying to identify the body. They just bundle the corpse into the police van and drive off.

PLOT 25

THE HOSPITAL
Chief is lying on the bed with an oxygen support system. His wife is seen with tears while the manager stands looking confused. It is at this stage that the spirit of chief comes in and enters the body. At the same time also he starts to breathe faster, shaking his body and trying to remove the oxygen support system.

Sister Mary—[*Very surprised*]

Oh my God he has regained consciousness.]

Chief Ogbuefi—[*holding the wife and looks at her in the face*]

Mary you're right God is real. Now I know I am the one that is a disgrace to the entire family.

[*At this stage the doctor comes in and is very surprised to see chief out of the bed. Chief turns to the doctor*].

Doctor I will be going to Enugu with the next available flight.

Doctor—[*Looks very confused*]

What do you mean Chief? I have made solid arrangement with some experts to perform some preliminary operation on you this evening.

Chief Ogbuefi—[*Looking at him straight in the face*]

I know you will not believe me. Heaven and Hell are real. I saw the two of them. Doctor do all you can to avoid Hell.

[*Turning to the manager*]

Go and settle the bill.

[*Turning to the wife. They looked at each other romantically*]

Doctor—[*Looks at them and waves his head, then he turns to the nurse and manager*]

Young man come let us prepare the bill for you.

[*They all go outside leaving chief and the wife alone*]

Chief Ogbuefi—[*Looking at her.*]

Mary I am really sorry for the embarrassment I've caused you and the children, will you forgive me especially when you hear the details of this episode.

Sister Mary—My dear I don't need any details. I am only happy to see the grace of God manifesting in you.

Chief Ogbuefi—Mary do you know what happened?

[*She just shakes her head again*].

That man Jesus Christ delivered me from going to hell. Do you now know something else? I will spend the rest of my life serving him.

Sister Mary—Oh my God! What a great miracle of the year.

[*This time she falls into the warm embrace of the husband, later she seems to have remembered something and disengages herself from him*].

What happened to our marriage? Remember you wanted me to choose between you and Christ whom to marry.

Chief Ogbuefi—[*Seems to catch the joke*]

Oh my God. Do you know what we are going now to the shop. I will get us a diamond ring to mark a new covenant marriage in Christ Jesus.

[*They hold each other in a very passionate kiss*].

SCENE 26

ULTIMATE CLUB
The two cars are seen moving into a big compound. The man in black suit comes out first and opens the door. Ebube is dragged into a temple like hall his two hands are tied behind. Chief Odobra goes to a door marked secret knocks 3 times and the door opens by itself. He goes into a room lit up with candles

of different colors. Seated in a semicircle are 5 men facing the Chief priest who sits behind the shrine?

Chief Priest—Oh Chief Odobra! We have been very concerned about the success of this operation. How is it going?

Chief Odobra—Very successful, I hope by tomorrow night the lamb for the sacrifice will be ready.

Chief Priest—I am sure you are all aware that the only hand to strike the boy first is that of the father. Remember Abraham was the one to raise his hand first to kill his only son. To avoid the pains of looking for another lamb Chief Ogbuefi must initiate his willingness to give the lamb to the Gods.

Chief Odobra—[*very confused*]

If he is not willing to do so, what then do we do? Our business enterprises are collapsing and every thing now depends on this sacrifice.

Chief Priest—Hold your breath. All things are possible to those who believe. If he fails to come willingly then he will do it unwillingly.

[*Laughing and pointing to a big drum*

This will bring him here.

[*He then beats the drum three times and a dwarfish muscular creature emerges from behind the shrine*]

He will show you where to keep the lamb safe.

[*With a smile*]

Don't worry by tomorrow every thing will be all right.

[*They all bow to him 3 times before being escorted by the dwarf. They go where Ebube lay on the floor.*]

Chief Odobra—Bring him and fellow us.

[*The dwarfish creature leads them through a passage to a room marked secret. He knocks 3 times with a horn like instrument on the door and it opens. They untied him and push him into a room that looks like a cell and lock him up.*]

SCENE 27

CHIEF OGBUEFI'S HOUSE

Juliet—Are you sure they have not killed Ebube? Why is God punishing us like this? How will life be in this house without Ebube? Oh my God what will mummy do? Can she survive without Ebube in this house? And daddy will he survive it? His entire struggle in life is to hand over his business to Ebube

[*She weeps as her sister comes and places her hand on her shoulder to console her.*]

[*The two girls are seated and weep silently*]

Nkechi—Don't worry Julie my God is a living God. When all hopes are lost, he must be trusted.

Juliet—How can we trust God in a situation like this?

[At this stage they were both weeping uncontrollably as the doorbell rang they stop in fright and hesitate to open the door until they heard the gate man's voice.

Aboki—its me Aboki*!*

Nkechi ran and opened the door for Aboki the security man and a police officer.]

Aboki—Haba—All of you stop crying. Police don come.

Police officer—Ok girls stop crying. What and what did they take from you?

Juliet—They kidnapped our brother.

Police Officer—[*surprise*] kidnapped?

Aboki—yes sir. They cariam put am inside white 504 saloon car comot.

Police Officer—Did they take any other thing?

Nkechi—We are not sure.

Police Officer—Can you recognize any of them if you see them?

Nkechi—They were all masked.

Police Officer—Okay follow me outside.

[They follow him to a police van outside the compound. Inside the van 4 police men with guns.]

Unveil the corpse

[The two girls shout and hold each other when they see the corpse]

Can you recognize any of them.

Juliet—Yes!

[still hiding her face]

I recognize the big belt and red turtle neck polo shirt. He even used the belt on me.

Police Officer—Very well. We have them all in our net.

Nkechi—How about my brother?

Police Officer—We will find him. Okay?

[He just leaves them and goes into the van]

Let's go back to the station. Our case is a kidnap case. We must question these suspects thoroughly. I believe the money found with them is the ransom but by whom and for what reason is our next assignment.

[At this stage the airport taxi carrying Chief and his wife drives into the compound. Chief comes out first and goes straight to the police while the wife rushes to the daughters.

Sis. Mary—What is going on?

[*She holds them together*]

Where is Ebube?

Juliet—Armed robbers came to our house and kidnapped him.

[*She starts to weep and wail uncontrollably. While the two daughters are trying to console and protect her from falling, Chief just lay his weight on the car bonnet. The police officer goes to him and helps him stand up*

Police Officer—[*still holding him*]

Chief listen this is a kidnap case and is always very delicate. Take your wife and daughters inside and wait for their call. Even your best friend should not be told. If they make any demand this is our mobile number.

[*Giving him a piece of paper*]

If you make any mistake it will backfire and you will never see your son again.

[*He goes into the van and they drive off*] *Chief wipes his face with handkerchief. He goes to his wife and daughters and takes them inside. At this stage they are all weeping uncontrollably. He just leaves them and goes to settle the airport taxi driver.*

SCENE 28

IN THE SPIRIT WORLD
[With special effect the territorial spirit is with her special aides]

Territorial Spirit—I want to have the privilege of watching the destruction of Chief Ogbuefi Akulue

[With the same effect Ogbuefi is seen in the screen been escorted into hell fire by two demons.

Territorial Spirit—*[Pointing to the screen]*

Yes that son of a bitch. I really want to see his end.

[She laughs]

That will serve as a deterrent to any one who may want to follow his footsteps.

[This time her countenance changes completely. She sits up anger written all over her face. She sees Jesus Christ in pure white clothe blocking the entrance to the pit, blood gushing out from his two hands, feet, and rib.

Territorial Spirit—*[With anger]*

You again what have you got to do with that sinner? He belongs to us.

[This time her face looks very terrible]

You cost us this agony. You never gave us chance of repentance.

[*She is so angry that she starts to destroy things in her palace. She goes straight to the agent operating the screen and throws her out*]

I don't want to see that blood again. Get out of my face.

[*This time the whole palace goes into flame and smoke fills everywhere.*

SCENE 29

CHIEF'S HOUSE
The wife and daughters appear in agony.

Sister Mary—My dear for how long must we wait for their call.

Chief Ogbuefi—I know people whom I feel might know something about this business but let us wait till dusk and see what will happen.

[*This time he picks up the phone and calls the police*]

Yes /officer this is Chief Ogbuefi. Any information concerning my son? No call. No demand yet. So the suspects have not mentioned any name. I might be of help to you okay? But for how long? Thank you.

[*He drops the phone*]

They said the suspects have given them useful information. Let's continue to pray and wait.

[At this stage the door bell rings Juliet goes and opens the door for Johnny and two other students from the university. They go straight to Chief Ogbuefi and greet him. Johnny who stands as the leader of the group speaks on behalf of the rest.

Johnny

Since my last visit to this place my friends here and I have not failed in praying for your family and especially Ebube. In the campus a roommate is like a blood relation though he does not share the same faith with me. I have every hope that one day he will come to know Christ and God will be revealed in him. Last night we were led by the spirit of God to organize a special night vigil on his behalf and now we are meant to understand bandits came here and kidnapped him. Well all I have to say to this is that God is faithful even when we are not faithful to him. Chief when we were at the peak of our prayer last night a word of prophecy came to us and was directed to you and that is the main reason we came today. The Holy Spirit fell on one of us and she spoke this word go give him my word in exodus 20 v4—5 Chief I will want one person in your family to read this passage.

[The wife goes and brings a bible and starts to read the

> *Voice—Exodus 20 vs. 4—5 Thou shall not make unto thee any graven image, or any likeness of any thing that is in heaven above or that is in the earth beneath, or that is in the water under the earth: Thou shall not bow down thyself to them; for I the Lord thy God am a jealous God. Visiting the iniquity of the fathers upon*

the children unto the third and forth generation of them that hate me.

SCENE 30

POLICE STATION
The suspects are all kept in different rooms undergoing interrogation on the whereabouts of the boy. They all deny knowledge of the kidnap and claim the money is for a business trip to Lagos for one of them. It is only when an electric boiler is about to be used on the private part of one of the youngest amongst them that he shouts

Suspect—[*In pain and agony*]

Please wait sir I will talk

SCENE 31

CHIEF ODOBRA'S HOUSE
The wife, his daughter and two sons are seen in their living room. The two boys are playing cards while Ify the daughter is seen watching a movie. Their mother and the maid are seen preparing the table for dinner.

Madam Odobra—Every body the food is ready.

[*They all leave whatever they are doing and go to the dinning table. When all are seated—*

Ike—[*With food in his mouth*]

Mummy what has been bugging dad lately?

Ify—He seems to be very aggressive now, yesterday he nearly threw me out of the window when I asked of money from him.

Michael—And he spends most of his time in the club.

Madam Odobra—[*Dropping her spoon*]

Please! Please! Leave your father alone and eat your food.

[*It is at this stage the door bell rings and the maid comes out from the inner room opens the door for three policemen in plain clothes*].

Police Leader—[*Showing his badge*]

Where is Chief Odobra?

Madam Odobra—He is not in the house now any problems?

Police Leader—Where can I find him?

Madam Odobra—I don't know. What is the problem?

Police Leader—Tell your husband if he comes back that he can get away with anything but killing a cop and kidnap he can't escape.

[*Turning to his men*]

Let's go.

Immediately they leave the room. One of them disappears into the backyard while the rest enter the car and drive off. As soon as they leave Ike his elder son runs to the window and looks.

Ike—Mummy they have gone

[*Picking up the phone*]

Let me call the club and tell him what is going on.

[*As he is dialing the number the police officer comes in through the backdoor and points a gun at him.*]

Police Officer—Drop that phone and where is the club?

Ike—I don't know.

Police Officer—[*Brings out a handcuff*]

Now you are going to the station with me.

[*He holds him and is about to handcuff him when the mother shouts*]

Madam Odobra—No! Leave him alone. It is at Ultimate Club.

Police Officer—Now listen all of you. This house is under surveillance. If you make any other silly mistake our orders is to shoot.

[*With that statement he leaves*]

SCENE 32

CHIEF OGBUEFI'S HOUSE
As the wife finishes reading the passage, Johnny continues—

Johnny—The word of God is spirit and is life. It is you alone who can give the current interpretation of this passage and how it relates to the present situation. The bible says we are not fighting against flesh and blood but against spiritual forces in the highest places. The only contribution we think we should make at this critical moment to our friend and roommate is to beg your permission to hold a night vigil in your house with members of your household.

Chief Ogbuefi—My son I am really thankful to God for showing me his abundance mercy. This is a very good opportunity for me to confess to my wife and children my involvement in secret cult. Now follow me

[*He leads them to his secret room and opens the door*].

I believe this is what God is talking about in that passage.

[*The room is decorated like a shrine with an altar in the center, a big cross turned upside down, different status from Indian and portraits of temple leaders from India and China. A big standing mirror, charms amulets and burning incense and many others.*]

To be frank I joined this group not to make money because I had enough before joining them but for protection of my life, my family and wealth. Now the very thing I called them to protect is the very thing they want to take away from me but God saw my foolishness and met me in the hospital.

There and then I saw the living Christ, the savoir of the world. Now I am going to do away with this rubbish.

[As he starts to dismantle them Johnny stops him]

Johnny—Before we do that we must first pray to God. First let us read

Acts 19vs 18—19 *and many that believed came, and confessed, and showed their deeds. Many of them also which used curious arts brought their books together and burned them before all men and they counted the price of them and found it fifty thousand pieces of silver.*

[After reading this passage he starts to pray]

SCENE 33

CLUBHOUSE

[The shrine is decorated with curious arts. Members are seen standing round a big casket in their animal skin uniform. The priest is behind the shrine beating the big drum at intervals. Two strong men bring Ebube into the arena. He is moving like a person under the influence of drug. They lay him inside the casket. The priest continues to beat his drum at intervals. There is silence and tension. Suddenly the drum stops.

The Chief Priest—This method of invitation to any member to perform this ritual becomes necessary when that member is unwilling to do it consciously. The only difference is that—:

[He pauses]

Chief Ogbuefi Akulue Uno 1 will never be alive to disobey the club again. [*At this stage outside the building the police start to take their positions in strategic places around the club. Already some have entered the club. The club's security man is already in handcuff while inside the ceremony arena two warning shots are fired by the police.*

SCENE 34

CHIEF OGBUEFI'S HOUSE

After Johnny has finished praying he starts to sing a song—

There is power mighty in the blood. There is power mighty in the blood of JESUS CHRIST. There is power mighty in thy blood.

With this song they start to carry all the materials in the secret room to the burning fire they set outside. It is while they are doing this that the police van comes into the compound and stops. They all stop and watch them. Chief Ogbuefi leaves them and goes to the police. When they see Ebube coming out of the police van the whole place erupts into shouting and jubilation. The mother, sisters and friends leave what they are doing and run to him and lift him up. Even the police seem to be enjoying the scene.

THE END

WRITTEN BY
Jonathan Ezemeka

THE BLOOD AND THE COVENANT

PRELUDE

Lynda is a beautiful girl betrothed to the shrine of Ogbodu right from birth. Among the people of Edeani Ogbodu is worshiped as a God and no one ever lived to question his authority through his priests.

Fortunately or unfortunately Lynda came to know Jesus Christ just before the age of her final hand over to the shrine. To the people of this community Ogbundu is their tradition and it is sacred. Ogbondu is also their custom and is above every other thing. To question any decision of Ogbondu is sacrilege. The stage is now set for a terrible cosmic battle. THE BLOOD AND THE COVENANT.

SCENE 1

FLASH BACK
Before the Ogbondu river stands a very big shrine in a thick forest. From a very long distance approaching this shrine is Mazi Okwuonu leading a group of three. In his hand he holds a machete and a den gun. Behind him is

Lynda his daughter wearing traditional beads trying to keep pace with him.

Bringing up the rear end is Lynda's mother carrying a calabash of about two gallons on her head and holding a chicken in one hand.

At the entrance to the shrine we see the chief priest and about four members of the council of elders welcoming them with smiles into the shrine. When everyone is seated the chief priest starts to address them with these words.

Chief priest
[Beaming with smiles]

Mazi Okwuonu you are the true son of the soil. On behalf of all the members seated here I say again welcome. With the exception of this little girl here we were all living witnesses when Mazi Okwuonu and his wife came to Obgondu seven years ago for the seed of the womb. Today he has come to present the child to Ogbondu in accordance to the agreement made before us. I believe you have done the right thing. If you thank the gods for what they have done to you they will do more. Now let me see the materials. *[Mazi Okwuonu gives him the items which includes a chicken, two gallons of palm wine and three coins]*

[Other members get up one after the other to shake hands with him and to offer their congratulations]

The chief priest takes these items and places them on the altar. He kills the chicken and sprinkles the blood on the altar. He collects some wine and pours libation and made some incantations. After which he turns and starts to address them thus—

Chief Priest

Mazi Okwuonu the gods are very pleased with you and your family

[He kept silent for some time].

Your daughter has been chosen as a bride to the gods. According to the language of the spirits, Ogbondu has taken special interest in her and therefore on no account she should be given out for marriage. Before the age of womanhood she should be brought back here for the final ceremony.

[Mazi Okwuonu bows his head in shock while his wife starts to weep]

SCENE 2

17 YEARS LATER [LOSS ANGELES U.S.A.]
Johnny Scott and his wife Mary are sleeping on the bed when suddenly Johnny finds himself in a terrible nightmare. He sees himself led into this village by an angel. There he sees people in chains like slaves about to be exported. From a near by river comes one like the prince of a mermaid, accompanied by some terrible looking demons.

Prince

What are you doing in this village? This village and its people belong to me. You don't belong here. Therefore I am giving you just a minute to leave this place. Or you will be destroyed.

[Before Johnny can open his mouth to speak these ferocious looking demons pick him up like a baby doll and throw him into a valley. He rolls down the valley to the feet of one standing like the Son of a God. Johnny manages to sit up. He looks from the feet up and behold the Son of God standing before him with a bible in his hand.

VOICE

Whom shall I send and who will go for us.

After this Johnny wakes up with a start and sweating profusely. He is also panting like a dog.

Mary

{Surprised to see him in this state she holds him and helps him to sit up]

What is it? You are really frightening me.

[They hold each other very tight]

My dear what is wrong with you. You really frightened me.

Johnny

[Gradually disengaging himself from her]

Well it is like a dream but it looks real. I was in this village some where in Asia or in Africa. I saw these people in chains both on their hands and feet. Oh my God it was a pathetic sight. When they saw me, oh it was as if salvation has come to them. I saw it in their faces but suddenly one like the prince of mermaid appeared from nowhere with terrible looking demons. They bundled me like a sack of wheat and threw me down a valley. When I got up behold it was Jesus Christ himself standing before me with a bible. Some how I heard his voice like thunder saying whom shall I send.

{He turns and looks directly into her eyes

My dear I think God is now confirming my call for a mission in African or Asia.

[The moment he said that Mary leaves him on the bed and sits on the chair]

What is wrong with what I have just said?

Mary

Do you want us to start quarreling over that issue again? I think I have made myself clear on that, if you really want to go you can go but count me out. It is your dream, not mine. Do you think our God is an author of confusion? We are just married and you think He wants us to go and die in the jungle because you had nightmare. You have hared stories of missionaries who went to Africa and Asia and how most of them ended their journey. The vision to me should wait after we might have finished raising our kids or do you expect our babies to be raised in the jungle also?

Johnny
[Very confused and showing a great sign of surprise]

Do you mean we should stay even if it is the will of God? In Jeremiah 10: 23. The word of God says it is not given to a man to dictate his steps. Remember before we got married I told you I have a mission call but I can't tell the place and you said it is okay with you, now what is happening.

Mary
Nothing I just think I am part of you

[Tears rolling down her cheeks]

I feel I am a human being also, If it is the will of God. Then I should know too. The dream or vision is not mine but yours. Such an important issue that got to deal with our future must be convincing to both of us. In spiritual mathematics 1+1=1.

[After saying that, she goes straight to bed while Johnny sits on the bed resting his head on his hands.]

SCENE 3

MARY'S OFFICE
Mary is in her office operating a computer. At one stage she stops working while her mind goes straight to the event of last night with her husband. [With special effects some

of these clips will be shown] After a while she comes to her senses and starts operating on the computer. On the screen what she sees catches her attention. She becomes frightened when she sees one like the prince of mermaid in the screen behind this spirit she sees some terrible looking demons ready to strike. At the end of this scene she sees people in chains crying for help. She cries out and runs out of the office throwing the computer and table down. The noise she made attracted attention. Members of the company she works for come out and some how manage to calm her down.

Mary
[Looking very frightened, screaming and at the same time pointing at the computer.]

I saw them they are there.

The Manager.
Who are they?.

[With the help of some members of the staff they pick up the table and the computer.

The Manager
[Switches on the computer]

The computer is ok, what did you see that really frightened you.

[With a smile]

Okay every body back to work. You know she is just back from honeymoon. I am now giving you another week off at least to see a doctor to check the amount of honey in the moon.

[The whole staff bursts into laughter. When all have gone Edina her friend in the church remains.

Edina
Mary what is wrong with you? You've caused a lot of confusion.

Mary
Oh my God I hope I am not going crazy.It is this mission issue with my husband.

Edina
So two of you have not settled that issue with God in prayer and what happened?

Mary
It was late last night-

[With special effect clips of that vision is replayed]

And this morning right here in my office I saw the same thing in my computer.

Edina
If what you saw in the computer relates to your husband's vision then the message is clear God has just confirmed it to you. Please stop resisting the work of God.

[She held her hand

Let us pray that God gives you the wisdom and the strength to do his will]

SCENE 4

Mary is rearranging and at the same time collecting some of her materials that were scattered all over the places. After which she begins to work on the computer again. It is at this stage Johnny her husband walks into the office full of panic

Johnny

My dear what is wrong? Your manager called. He says I should take you to the hospital. *[Mary gets up and they held each other for a very long time] [There is a knocking at the door that separates them from each other Mary left him to open the door for the mail bearer who hands her a letter and leaves.*

Mary
[She takes it and gives to her husband]

This is for you.

Johnny
[Taking the letter from her]

It is from the World Mission Outreach Inc.

[Opening the letter and reading at the same time.

Mary
What are they saying?

Johnny
They claim that after spirited prayer we have been selected to serve the Lord as missionaries in a village called Edeani in West Africa. And that we are given up to two weeks from now to accept or reject the offer through the board's secretary general

[He hands the letter over to her. She reads through it and then looks up to him]

. I believe we have come to the end of our debate on this issue now what do we do?. *[Johnny looks at her directly in the eyes}*

Do we say yes to God or no to him?

Mary
They look at each other for a very long time it is Mary who speaks first

I will go with you.

Johnny
[Surprised] Really?

He takes her in his arms and they hold each other for a very long time.

SCENE 5

This scene shows their departure from the J.F.K.International airport. Edina and a handful of friends see them off. It also shows their arrival at the Muritala Mohammed International airport. From this place they board another local flight that takes them to Enugu local airport. One Ebenizer who serves as the leader in the church meets them at the arrival hall. He leads them to board a mini bus to Edeani village. The bus is very crowded with people going to the big Edeani market. Johnny and his wife are privileged to occupy the front seats alone while Ebenizar is in the back seat with their luggage. The journey took them two hours through rough roads stopping at different villages to drop and pick up passengers. Finally the bus stops at Edeani village square where a handful of converts are waiting to welcome them. They are taken to a mud house in the church compound. It is a single bedroom, a living room with outside toilet and kitchen. It is very neat and airy. The furniture inside is very simple a cane chair, cane bed and tables. When everyone is settled it is Ebenizer who makes a welcome speech.

Bro. Ebenizer

Sir you are welcome to Edeani When the news came to us about your coming we prayed that God would grant you a merciful journey. I thank God for making your journey a success. As you may want to know this mission was established by Rev. Lovington who now lives at Enugu overseeing many mission centers across the region. This community is very accommodating but very resistant to the gospel. Even Lovington himself could not explain why after so many years of mission activity the people of Edeani seems to have built a wall protecting them against the word of God. This center is mostly made up of people regarded as untouchable or the outcast. This I believe makes it impossible for the real children of the soil to come to the church. To the villagers the mission is simply regarded as the religion of the outcast.

Today at least we are happy to welcome you for it has always been our prayer to have a white Missionary in our midst. This of course will boost our public image and destroy the concept that the religion is for the outcast. To let them know we are worshiping the true God. Your presence here has given a new life to the church and to every one of us. For many years we have prayed for a white missionary in Edeani. I know it is going to be very difficult for you and this your beautiful wife, but nevertheless be assured that we will not stop in praying for you. Therefore on behalf of the people of Edeani I welcome you and your wife.

Johnny

Thank you Bro. Ebenezer for the hospitality and the enlightenment, from what you have just said we are now very convinced God planned this mission for us. I am also very convinced that he who began this good work will bring it to perfection to his own glory. Now I want you to pass a message to every member of the church and to the villagers as well that I will want to speak to them. Tell them there is going to be a film show.

Bro. Ebenezer

They will surely come at least to see the white man and his wife.

Johnny

Let us pray.

SCENE 6

THE CHURCH COMPOUND
At this inaugural meeting to welcome the new missionary and his wife many villagers came at least to watch the Jesus film while others came to see the white man and his wife.

Johnny

My name is Johnny Scott and this is my wife Mary. We are here today not by our own power or design but by the grace of God. I am happy to see that most of you are touched by the film Jesus Christ of Nazareth. First of all, God has given every one of us this special opportunity to become his real children through his son Jesus Christ. There are two types of birth—

[1] Birth through flesh. Every human being is born into flesh which is through the mating of male and female. By this we are all born into sin. Psalm 51:5 the bible says in sin we are born and in sin we are conceived. The penalty for sin is eternal death. The greatest sin today is man's rejection of the gift of God, which is Jesus Christ.

Romans 6:23 For the wages of sin is death; but the gift of God is eternal life through Jesus Christ our Lord.

[2] The second type of birth is spiritual birth, Jesus Christ died on the cross as you've just seen to give us this kind of life. No one can become a child of God without first been born into the spirit. How do we do that? Simple! Just believe sincerely in your heart that his death and resurrection has made you clean before God. Then God has no alternative but to give you the power to become His sons and daughters. God is spirit and any one who must worship Him must do so in spirit and in truth. Jesus Christ is the way the truth and the life no one can see God without Him. Tomorrow might be too late for you. Today might be the only chance you have. If you really want to become a child of God you are free to come out. I will pray a special prayer for you

[A handful of people came including Lynda.

Music—Unto Jesus I surrender—Unto him I freely give—I surrender—I surrender all
I surrender I surrender all

SCENE 7

Lynda returns home from the church in the company of another three girls who are converts. At home she sees her father having a deep discussion with Ogbondu chief priest and his council of elders. The girls greet them and go to the backyard to greet Lynda's mother. The men stop

their discussion to return their greetings and continue after making sure the girls are not within hearing range.

Chief Priest

Mazi Okwuonu You know exactly what I am saying the girl is 17 and next year she will enter womanhood. This is the covenant you made with the gods 10 years ego. She is a bride to the gods and must spend 4 market days to the service of the shrine to prepare her for the final ceremony.

Elder 2

You know everything I hope the religion of the outcast has not entered your brain.

Mazi Okwuonu

[Shocked and surprised]

I now remember it has really been a very long time indeed. I am still wondering how this custom could have effected her now at this time. Things have changed a lot she spends most of her time in the mission and school.

[Looks very helpless and confused]

.Well I promise to talk things over with her. I will persuade her to see reason.

Chief Priest

It is better you do more than that. The issue at stake is a delicate one.

[With that statement they leave his house]

Mazi Okwuonu sits down speechless. With special effect the incident at the shrine with himself, Lynda and his wife is relayed to him. He comes to his senses when Lynda called his attention to receive her friends.

Lynda

My friends in the church have come to greet you.

Mazi Okwuonu

[He seems not to notice them]

Lynda please sit down I want to talk to you.

[He just waves to the girls]

Okay my daughters.

Lynda

Daddy is anything wrong?

Mazi Okwuonu

Yes everything seems to be wrong now. You know these men that have just left.

Lynda

.Yes, the Ogbondu council of elders, is anything wrong?

[This time Lynda's mother comes in]

Mazi Okwuonu

Do you know why everybody calls you queen.

Lynda
[Shakes her head]

No.

Mazi Okwuonu
10years ego there was a covenant made at Ogbondu shrine in the presence of these men to hand you over to the shrine when you reach womanhood. Your mother here is a living witness to what I am saying. We have no choice Ogbondu does his selection. Who am I to question the decision of the gods.

Lynda's Mother
[Looks shocked and surprised]

Is that why they came? Things have changed since then and what did you tell them?

Mazi Okwuonu
What do you expect me to tell them. You know everything. When we were looking for a child we consulted the gods through them and 10 years ego when the covenant was made you witnessed everything I want us to reason together as a family. What should we do?

Lynda
Daddy! Wait a minute, you mean you want me to go and live like those outcast women parading themselves as sacred wives to the gods. Their children are roaming about the village as bastards. You mean I should become like one of them? God forbids. I am now a child of God and the blood of Jesus Christ covers me.

Mazi Okwuonu

Many have tried to escape but how far did they get. This covenant is far different from what you are talking about. To even think of breaking it is death.

[At this stage Lynda's mother bursts into tears]

[Lynda goes to her while the father leaves them and goes to his room.

SCENE 8

Lynda is in her room reading the bible when her mother walks in she is still in tears. They keep silent for a very long time before she speaks.

Mother

Since these men left our home I have not been able to concentrate on any thing. I am totally confused and I feel guilty concerning the situation we have put you into. Since I was born and now I am old I have never seen anyone break this covenant with the shrine and live. You are my only child I prefer you alive in the shrine than to weep daily in your graveside. When a woman is in dire need of a child like I was she becomes irrational. Your father and I were to blame. We did not consider the consequences all we wanted was just a baby. Please my daughter you must prepare to spend the four market days in the shrine to save your life and ours.

Lynda

[Picking up her bible]

Mother, do not fear them but just listen—

Voice
Luke 12:4—5 And I say unto you my friends be not afraid of them that kill the body and after that have no more that they can do. But I forewarn you whom you shall fear. Fear him which after he hath killed hath power to cast into hell yea I say unto you fear him.

/Listen to another word mother/

Voice
Luke 9:24 For whosoever will save his life shall loose it but whosoever will loose his life for my sake the same shall save it
[She then closes the bible]

Mother which one do you want us to accept. The Ogbondu shrine or the word of God. I would rather die than accept their verdict. I can not be a slave to satisfy the sexual urge of these wizards. My body is the temple of God.

Mother
It seems that the bible has gotten into your head. How do you think words written in pages of papers can save you from the anger of Ogbondu? Look at Angelina who roams the market place naked. Look at Elechi also naked in the same market place. They are just two among many who tried.

[It is at this stage they hear knocking on the door. Lynda gets up to open the door for Bro. Ebenizer, Johnny, Mary and an old lady popularly known as Ada Jeso but her real name is Sis Odinaka

Sister Odinaka
[Very impatient]

My daughter you know my story in this village I was enslaved to this shrine when I was your age. Now look at me I am old enough to be your grand mother but nothing in life to show as a woman. I know the evil your parent's wants to force you into. I can't say why but I believe God has placed the burden on me to tell you to take courage and never yield to their demand.

[At this stage Mazi Okwuonu comes in, anger written all over his face he seem s to control his anger when he sees the white man and his wife.

Johnny
[Moving straight to shake hands with him]

I am Johnny Scott the new missionary, here is my wife Mary. I believe you are Lynda's father we have come to talk with you.

[Lynda goes inside and brings some cane seats for them to sit on.]

Yes I really understand the terrible situation you are in. The church members have briefed me on what is going on. I am fully aware Lynda is your only child I can understand the kind of love you people have for her. Now if I may ask you this question Mazi If for example the gods of this land decides to kill your daughter or use her for sacrifice will you be willing to stand in far her.

Mazi Okwuonu
Do you mean if I will be ready to die for my daughter?

Johnny

Yes.

Mazi Okwuonu
[He keeps silent for some time]

Well that time has not come yet.

Johnny
Yes I know why I am asking you this question I did not come into this village because I wanted to or because I enjoy it. I came because Jesus Christ who gave his life for me and for you asked me to come into this village to bring you people the good news of freedom. Freedom from the powers of Satan and his agents like Ogbondu and other gods you fear. All that is required of you is to believe that and you will be free. God in his mercy gave us an opportunity to escape this fear of death which Ogbondu and his group are using against you and your family. Jesus is the only one who can save you and your family from this problem. Just trust him and see.

Mazi
[Shaking his head]

What is at stake is far bigger than your belief. Ogbondu is not a man he does what he likes. To question his decision is death. I want to ask you my own question did your church members take you around the village square.

Johnny

What is there in the Market Square?

Mazi

You will see one or two naked women roaming the market. They tried to question the authority of Ogbondu

[With special effect these naked women will be shown as they roam the market square begging for food and making funs]

You are talking of what is in the pages of a paper but I am talking from personal experience. Ogbondu did not come to us we went to him and made this covenant. All they want from us is to keep our promise. My wife and I are to blame for this mess. We were desperately in need of a child and now they want the child back when we needed her most

[He weeps silently]

[At this stage they start to hear the noise of drums and a gong coming to the compound]

Johnny

What is going on?

Mazi

I believe it is the first peaceful message from the shrine. The native doctor masquerade will come first to plead the return of Ogbondu's maiden.

[The women run into the rooms while the men including Mary go outside to meet the group. This time they are already inside Okwuonu's compound. Mazi Okwuonu goes straight and kneels before the masquerade.

Masquerade

[Very haggard looking, ugly and walks with a walking stick like an old man. Half a dozen men who accompany him stand behind]

My son rise for I come in peace

[He uses the horse tail in his hand to pat at Mazi Okwuonu's back.]

[This time one of the attendants brings a stool for him to sit on which he does with great effort].

My son any person the god wants to kill they first make him mad. I came in peace. Obey the gods and live.

[At this stage he raises his stick high as one trying to place curse on some one but this time his voice becomes very high and aggressive]

My son it is with great pain that I have left the land of the dead to intercede on your behalf. My feet will never touch this soil again

[Pointing his walking stick on the ground this time he points the stick directly at him]

Next week market day is your last day to present the girl to the shrine.

[He gets up and starts to move outside the compound after a moment he stops and points his stick at Johnny]

White man! He who learns the songs of the birds should also learn how they fly.

[With that statement he leaves the compound with his entourage]

[They all stand speechless until the masquerade and his entourage leaves then they all go back to their discussion.

Johnny
What does he mean by what he just told me?

Mazi
I told you we talk practical things and you talk of words. How then do you explain this ugly creature. Can your bible describe the masquerade itself? Tell me. From now on every person associated with my daughter is an enemy of Ogbondu. She is now seen as untouchable. No scene man will ever marry her from this village and beyond. For my wife and I to escape the anger of the gods we must present her to the shrine on or before the next market day or go to the shrine and disassociate ourselves from her action. Every member of your church knows

about this that the presence of this ugly creature in my compound shows Lynda is the property of Ogbondu. Any man who takes her, as a wife will be destroyed by Ogbondu. From the people's point of view she is married to the gods of the land. Who is that god that will save her from the power of Ogbondu? Ogbondu is our custom and it is sacred , Ogbondu is our tradition and is above all things to question him is sacrilege.

[This time he starts to weep silently]

I want my daughter alive not a mental showcase.

Johnny
Please Mazi it is okay I want to make one request from you will you give this Jesus Christ a chance to prove himself to you?

Mazi
Okay I will, but how?

Johnny
I will just pray and hand you and your family over to God Is that okay?

[Mazi Okwuonu nods his head.]

I believe he will intervene before the deadline. Before we pray I want us to read

Voice—[1] Isaiah 28:18 And your covenant with death is disannulled and your agreement with hell shall not stand.

It is true you got yourself and family involved into this agreement but the word of God says every agreement you made with death has been destroyed. Do not fear them just believe this word. We are going to pray and ask God to reveal himself to you I believe that between now and next market day He will intervene Let us pray.

SCENE 9

Mazi Okwuonu is lying on his bed. He seems to be having a nightmare because he is turning from one corner of the bed to another. In the dream he finds himself in a hall that looks like a temple. In this hall, he sees members of the Ogbondu council of elders standing beside a bamboo stick bed. From the distance he sees a girl lying on the bed. Half of her body is covered with a white cloth, her hands and legs are tied to the bed. He moves nearer so he can see clearly. This time a small door on the side opens and the Chief priest himself comes out with a life cobra in his hand. The drum beats at interval while he continues to dangle and tap the head of the cobra. The chief priest raises his left hand and the drum stops. He starts to make incantations. He raises the head of the cobra towards the chest of the girl and rubs it down. He starts to speak to the girl in a strange language. At this stage the girl stands up and behold it is Lynda his daughter. He shouts at the top of his voice and wakes up. The noise he made attracts his wife and daughter, who rush into his room and see him sweating and gasping for air.

Lynda's Mother
[*She helps him to sit up*]

Mazi what is wrong with you?

Mazi Okwuonu
Lynda where are you? Are you okay?

Lynda
Daddy I am. What is wrong with you, you have disturbed the night.

Mazi Okwuonu
Lynda My daughter you will never go to that shrine even if it means death to me

SCENE 10

THE SPIRIT WORLD.
In the palace of the prince of Ogbondu, at the crown head of the Atlantic Ocean and the controller of the eastern gateway is the prince himself and some of his special aids.

Special Agent—
When will I go into the world and what will be my mission?

The Prince
I know you want to explore the world be careful the world is not as sweet as we see it from this realm. The human body you are to use is still under contention for your mission is to [1] to steal [2] to destroy and [3] to kill the word any where it is planted in this territory

Special Agent
[Full of surprise]

Who contends with the crown prince of Ogbundu? Can an egg challenge a rock? Who is that my lord? Let me your little slave destroy him and his family. You the prince of thunder, tell me who is he or her?. A spirit or man

[kneels down before his master]

Now my lord, tell me.

Prince
Now I will give you a little assignment

[Using special effect he reveals a screen on the wall showing Johnny and his wife in worm kissing and discussion. The agent seems to be in a hurry to leave]

Take it easy, these people are your problem to the outside world, your only hope to explore the world is to stop their mission in this territory. Now you can go.

[She immediately turns into bat and flies off.]

SCENE 11

Ebuka the first son of Chief Adaka the warrant chief of Edeani is riding on his bicycle. He comes across Lynda going to the mission for bible study. Ebuka turns his cycle towards her direction, overtaking and stooping in front of her. Lynda is very surprised but manages a smile.

Ebuka
[Returning the smile also]

. I am Ebuka may I know your name.

Lynda
I am Lynda and you are the son of Chief Adaka the one they say is going to be a lawyer soon.

Ebuka
Oh my God, you seem to know more about me but this is my first time of seeing you in this village. Where are you going?

Lynda
I am going to the church.

[They look at each other for a long time Lynda is the first to turn her face away]

I am going, I am already late.

Ebuka
You don't want me to come with you to the church?

Lynda
If I invite you will you come? Okay I now invite you to our night vigil tonight.

Ebuka
[Looks at her with great admiration]

Maybe next time.

[He turns his bicycle and leaves][Lynda watches him for some time and goes her way.

SCENE 12

Johnny and wife are visiting the enclave of the outcast community which is nearer to the main shrine of Ogbondu. In his company is Ebenezer the interpreter and a handful of church members including Lynda. Johnny was using this opportunity to distribute gifts of shirts, pencils, chalk, food and many other items.

Johnny
Make sure you all come for the night's vigil

[As he gives out the gifts to each person he invites them for the vigil.] Mary the wife is doing the same thing. It is at this stage Johnny notices a group of men just a short distance from the shrine sitting around a burning fire. He draws the attention of Bro. Ebenezer to himself.].

Who are these people?

Bro. Ebenizer
These are the Ogbondu council of elders.

Johnny
Take me to them I want to introduce myself to them.

They all go to the shrine where they met them eating roasted goat.

Johnny

I bring you all good tiding in the name of Jesus Christ. My name is Johnny Scott, this is my wife we are the missionaries in charge of the church. Our mission is to bring the good news of freedom to the people of Edeani, freedom from the powers of sin and from the powers of darkness.

[*It is at this stage people start to run helter scatter Johnny stops and looks. Behold it is a very big cobra coming towards them. Even the elders look frightened and stand up in fright Johnny stands his ground while the others disperse.*

Johnny

I rebuke you in the name of Jesus.

[*The big snake stands it ground just a stone throw from where Johnny stands. After a moment it lowers its head and starts to decay. Already flies start to fill every where. This time the council of elders comes near to the scene.*

Chief Priest

Abomination! Abomination!

Other Members

Abomination! They have killed the sacred snake. Abomination!

Ebenezer

[*Takes Johnny by his hand*]

Lets leave here immediately. To them it is an abomination to kill or harm the snake.

Johnny

But I did not touch the snake, it is the power of God.

Ebenizer

[Almost dragging him out of the compound]

If the villagers arrive you'll not be alive to explain that.

[Already people are starting to stamped out of the shrine. In this period of confusion Johnny and members of the church leave the scene.

SCENE 13

It is at this point while Lynda is rushing home from the scene of the incident that she meets Ebuka on her way back. He stops the cycle in front of her.

Ebuka

What is wrong? Who is chasing you?

Lynda

Ogbondu snake is killed and every person is running home.

Ebuka—

Who did that?

Lynda—
The villagers claimed the white man is responsible but
I know he did not touch the snake. It was the power of
God that killed the snake.

Ebuka
Oh well what has it got to do with you and I

[She looks at him with surprise]

Okay come let me take you home

*[Before she is able to say anything he lifts her up to sit at
the front bar of the bicycle. They look at each other but
Lynda is quick to turn her face]*

Now which way do I go.

*[Lynda gives him the direction, which he follows. They
come to a small cottage house she gives him the sign to
stop which he does. She comes down and is about to go
when Ebuka calls her back.*

Ebuka
[He looks at her with great admiration]

When will you take me to that your church?

Lynda
[This time she looks at him with great interest]

Do you really mean it.

[Ebuka nods his head]

We are supposed to hold a night vigil tonight, I don't know if the incident at the shrine will effect it.

Ebuka
Then tonight I will come to collect you, if it holds we go if not then I will go home. Is that okay with you?

[She hesitates for some time and then nods her head. They look at each other for a very long time.

Lynda
Thank you she turns and left

SCENE 14

Lynda goes in to greet her mom who seems to have watched the whole scene from within.

Lynda's Mother
Is that not Chief Adaka's son?

Lynda
Yes he is.

Mother
I can see he has taken special interest in you, remember nothing will ever make him to marry you because of Ogbondu.

Lynda

Oh Mummy who is talking about marriage now, he just saw me on the way and decided to take me home

Mother

But we saw the way you two looked at each other. Are you in love with him? And why did he bring you home.

Lynda

We were running home to avoid being lynched by the villagers.

Mazi Okwuonu

Why?

Lynda

Ogbondu snake has been killed. They claim the white man did it.

Both Parent

Abomination!

Mazi Okwuonu

What a terrible blunder to kill the snake is like killing Ogbondu himself. The church will pay seriously for it. First they will finance the funeral. Secondly the white man will shave his head and put on black as a sign of respect and he is expected to mourn for the snake at least 6 months. This incident is going to make things worse for us. Today supposed to be the last day you are to appear before the shrine. What do we do? Just sit and wait?

Lynda
Daddy what do you think will happen?

Mazi—
In a situation like this you can not sit down and determine the outcome, every thing depends on the reaction of the white man and the church. If they react negatively to the demands of the people then the Ebulebu masquerade will go into action and in such a situation many unpredictable things might happen.

Lynda's Mother
Like what?

Mazi—
Well they may decide to go on rampage burning the church or even to some extent killing. What I mean is that in an uncontrolled situation like this you can't just say. Let us just sit and wait,

Lynda
Daddy you said the other day that you would rather die than to see me go to the shrine why did you say that?

Mazi
[He just looks at her and his mind goes back to that dream] [Using special effects a clip of that dream is relayed].

Lynda
Daddy are you with us?

Mazi Okwuonu
[Lynda's voice brings him back to reality]

Well! Em. I don't really know or in short I can't just say, it is over my dead body I will see that happen.

Lynda
You know why I am saying this is that you can't stand alone to fight them You must take a stand either you are for the god of Ogbondu or for the God of the white man. The white man wants you and mummy to come for the vigil tonight. He wanted to come himself but I promised him I will invite you.

Mazi Okwuon
[He keeps silent for a while]

You are right my daughter we can not stand alone in this battle. We must stick together.

SCENE 15

THE SPIRIT WORLD
The prince of Ogbondu is surrounded by his special agents in his palace. They seem to be awaiting the return of the one that went on a mission.

The Prince
[Full of anger]

What is the latest news concerning Ichanga.

First Agent

The snake body she used died and decayed in the presence of the people.

Second Agent
No one can really tell her whereabouts. One thing is certain she escaped the fire.

[It is at this stage Ichanga bursts into the palace like a football. She is totally shattered like a mad woman panting seriously like a dog].

The Prince—
What happened? Didn't I tell you. The world is not an easy place for us now. Our time is running out.

[He turns and seems to be talking to a far object]

Even in this isolated place, the heat of that son of a bitch is disrupting our operations.

[He turns back to face his agents]

You are all bunches of fools so you are not able to read the handwriting on the wall.

[This time he starts to kick their asses one after the other]

Get out of my way move mobilize the people against that missionary and his church destroy them, put confusion in their midst.

[As he is speaking there is great thunder lightening and a heavy down pour. These evil spirits are at the same time turning themselves one after the other into very big bats and flying away].

SCENE 16

At the same time the voice of the village town criers are heard calling on all able bodied men of Edeani to assemble at the village square.

> *Voice*
> *Abomination! Abomination! Abomination!*
> *All taxable adults of Edeani should gather at the village square now, there is an abomination in this village. Abomination! Abomination! Abomination!.*

[He continues to make this announcement despite the heavy downpour while villagers are running to the Village Square] [The whole scene is in a state of confusion]

SCENE 17

IN THE CHURCH
The church members and a handful of villagers gather for the vigil. The whole place is alive with spirit filled songs and praises. Ebuka the chief's son is there, so are Lynda's parent.

> *Songs—That name is higher—above all other names—His name is Jesus—His name is Lord*

> *His name is higher—above all other names—His*
> *name is Jesus—His name is Lord.*

[The songs are very inspirational even Ebuka joins other young men in dancing to the music.][Lynda is in the choir section admiring him and really watching every move he makes]

[Johnny and his wife are seen also dancing to the music. The whole place is lively].

Johnny

[Johnny who stands with Ebenezer his interpreter raises his hand to stop the music for his message]

Let us pray. Father almighty I commit this moment into your great hand. I ask for your divine presence in our midst. Anoint your word and let it have an entrance in our lives.—In the name of the Father, the Son, and the Holy ghost. Amen.

> *Ephesians 6:10—12 . . . . .*
> *Voice—Put on the whole amour of God, that yea may be able to stand against the wiles of the devil. For we wrestle not against flesh and blood but against principalities, against powers, against the rulers of the darkness of this world, against spiritual wickedness in the highest places*

Two months before I came to Edeani. I was dreaming one night and suddenly found myself in this village I saw people bound in chains for destruction. From the river came one like a prince of mermaid accompanied by terrible looking demons. This evil spirit asked me to get out of this village because according to him the village and its inhabitants belong to him, before I could open my mouth to alter a word. They bundled me like a sack of wheat and threw me down into a valley. I rolled and rolled down the valley to the feet of a man. When I looked up behold it was Our lord Jesus Himself standing before me with a bible in his hand. The next thing I heard was a voice that roared like thunder saying.

Voice :— Who shall I send and who will go for us.
Today the bible is telling us in this passage that our battle is not against flesh and blood but against spiritual beings acting behind the scene most of the time using human beings to accomplish their missions. Our problem today as a church is not with the Chief, Ogbondu council of elders, the villagers, or even the dead snake. Our battle is between that evil spirit stationed somewhere behind the scene using innocent people to oppose the gospel. Satan knows his time is up, he is fighting a lost battle. Fear not, they will gather against us but God will use their gathering to glorify his name.

Voice
Philippians 2:9—11—Wherefore God also hath highly exulted him and given him a name which is above every name that at the name of Jesus every knew should bow of things in heaven and things in earth and things under the earth. And that every tongue should confess that Jesus Christ is Lord to the glory God the Father.

[The whole congregation burst into singing, dancing and clapping of hands.

Songs—At the name of Jesus
At the name of Jesus
Satan must bow down [Repeat]
Oh—At the name of our mighty Jesus—Tell me
who can stand?
At the name of our mighty Jesus—Every knee must
bow down.

[It is at this stage the villagers led by the Ebulebu masquerades burst into the church destroying everything. Ebuka who sees them coming jumps the pew in the midst of the commotion to the choir section and grabs Lynda and smuggles her out through the window. The whole place is in total confusion smoke fills everywhere. From the pulpit where they stand Ebenezer and some elders of the church are able to smuggle Johnny and his wife through a door behind the vestry into a nearby bush].

SCENE18

[At a nearby bush where they are Lynda is crying. They are able to see the church go into flames]

Lynda

[Still weeping]

Oh my God did you see my parents.

[From where they hide the flame from the burning church building seems to be exposing them more. Ebuka grabs her and takes her further into the bush]

I want to go home maybe they went home.

Ebuka

You stay here let me go and find my bicycle.

Lynda

[She holds his hand]

No! Maybe they are still there. Let us go through this path.

[She leads the way through a narrow path in the bush to a bigger road that leads to their village. They walk in darkness for around twenty minutes. From the place they are they can hear noises of destruction, shouting and burning coming from the direction of Lynda's compound. The nearer they go the more convinced they are it is from Lynda's compound. This time she starts to weep uncontrollably but this time she found comfort in the powerful shoulder of Ebuka and like a zombie she is led out of the scene this time towards the road leading to Chief Adaka's compound. But this time Ebuka is leading the way.]

SCENE 19

From the bush where they are hiding Johnny, wife, Ebenezer and two other members of the church see the church go in flames including the small mud house for the missionaries.

Johnny
[This time it starts to rain]

Now what do we do? It is not advisable for us to venture into the church compound. Is there any nearby mission or police post where we can go this night?

Ebenezer
There is a catholic mission in the next village we can spend the night there. It is an hour's walk from here.

Johnny
[He goes to his wife and holds her closely to himself].

Remember God has called us to carry this burden for him. Your reward shall be great in heaven.

Mary
So is yours

[They hold each other under the rain for a passionate kiss. [They start to move forward saying goodbye to the other two members who decidto go back].

Johnny
Now, Ebenezer, tell me, what is this snake to the people? It seems the death of the snake inflamed the whole thing.

Ebenizer
To the people of Edeani, Ogbondu is the snake and the snake is Ogbondu. That snake does not appear in the public anyhow. It only appears in the public to grace

the presentation of its maiden to the shrine. Any other time signifies danger. To the people of Edeani the death of the sacred snake shows that the power protecting them is gone. Legend has it that the snake is as old as the world.

[This time Ebenizer stops and speaks directly to Johnny].

Don't you think God has accomplished your mission in this village].

Johnny

What do you mean?

Ebenizer—

Based on the dream you had before coming to this village.

[He keeps silent for short time]

I am having the feelings that Ogbondu cult, the shrine and its authority in Edeani is finished.

Mary

It is too early to say that now, personally I believe the main battle has just begun.

SCENE 20

After they walk for about 30miutes in the dark and under a heavy rain, Lynda weeps uncontrollably. Ebuka pulls his shirt, dries it and tries to use it to wipe her tears. This time they start to hear voices at a distance and the light from a powerful flash light coming towards them.

Ebuka

[Giving her a sign to keep quiet]

[This time he shouts at top of his voice]

Akilika! Akilika! Akilika!

Voices—Ebuka—Ebus—Ebuka

[Pulling her along]

Come let's us go. Akilika is the head of my father's bodyguards.

[This time they meet Akilika and two other men carrying machetes and den guns with two girls, Ebuka's younger sister and Nkechi his half sister.

Ada Aku
[Who runs to him]

Ebus! What happened? We have been looking for you all over the places some people say they saw you in the church.

Akilika
[Who comes nearer to where he stands and pulls him aside]

Who is the girl that took you to the church?

[Lynda is with Ebuka's sisters weeping. This time Akilika directs his flash light on her face]

I tell you something Ebuka, your own abomination is worst than that of the white man's.

Ebuka

What do you mean?

Akilika

You've committed, in short there is no adjective to describe your offence. This girl is the personal property of Ogbundu. Just like the snake.

[This time he starts to laugh when Nkechi Ebuka's half sister comes]

Nkechi

So Ebuka the first time you entered the church is to go and carry Ogbondu's wife.

Akilika

No wonder the whole place went ablaze. Now if I may ask, where, are you taking her to? Your father is looking for you.

Ebuka—

She has no where to go. Their house is already burnt down.

Akilika

Then send her to the shrine where she belongs.

Ebuka—

You are crazier than I thought.

[Thinks for a moment]

Now what do you think father will do if I bring her home.

Akilika

[Thinks for a moment]

Well, Chief Adaka Ogwumagana your father is a god of his own and very unpredictable You know he never agrees with Ogbondu council of elders. To him some how, their functions, seems to interfere with his position as the warrant chief of Edeani.

[This time he becomes more serious using his hand to show what he means]

Have you done it?

Ebuka

[Very angry]

Done what? Get out!

[Pushing him aside].

Akilika
[This time he laughs again and starts to sing a song]

Iba na—ime unuka duru—nwa—pastor gbala
Obu—ya—ka mma—Ma iba nime unaka duru
nwa pastor gbala na obu ya ka nma,
Which means—If you enter the church—just go for
the pastor's daughter—that is the best thing to do

Ebuka
You are very crazy

[He leaves him and goes straight to Lynda]

Come let us go.

Lynda
[Still very reluctant to go with him]

Where are we going?

[She takes him aside]

Please Ebuka I don't want to be the cause of problem between you and your family.

Ebuka
Don't worry you will spend the night with my junior sister Ada Aku then tomorrow we can help you find your parents. It is too late for you to wonder alone in the dark.

Ada Aku
[Comes in to where they stand and takes Lynda by the arm]

Don't worry you will spend the night with me

[Reluctantly she goes with them].

SCENE 21

At Ebeano catholic parish, Johnny his wife and Ebenezer are waiting in the morning to see the parish priest. Their wet clothes have been washed and ironed. They all look very fresh. When the priest came in they all stand up to shake hands with him.

Priest
Please be seated. I am sorry I could not meet with you last night. I have gone to sleep when the report came that there is a white missionary and his wife outside the gate seeking for a place of refuge. I hope my people took good care of you, this place is village so don't expect much.

Johnny
Oh no It was all right. We slept well. The most important thing is that our clothes are washed and ironed. In short I don't think Loss Angeles would have offered much. We are very grateful.

Priest
Now If I may ask. Why did you organize the killing of the sacred snake, these areas are full of such sacred

animals. In some areas it is the monkeys while in some it is the tortoise, vulture or green snake as the case might be. I want to read something from the word of God.

> *Voice—First Corinthians 9:19—20-For though I be free from all men yet have I made myself servant unto all, that I might gain the more.—And unto the Jews I became as a Jew, that I might gain the Jews, To them that are under the law as under the law, that I might gain them under the law.*

We need patience in this job we found ourselves without it how can you understand the people and be able to change their old belief. You are very lucky it is not in this community who are you to touch their monkey. They will lynch you.

Johnny
[Controlling his anger]

The report you got about the whole incident is wrong no one touched the snake. Who am I to kill such a big snake. You need to see it. I only challenged the snake with the name of Jesus and it died and started to decay. Ebenezer, my wife and so many other villagers were there and saw what happened.

Priest
[Starts to laugh]

My son this is my 30th years as a missionary in India, Latin America and now in this country I have never seen such things. No one will believe such fabrications in order to gain popularity. Now why didn't you speak the same word when the villagers came? God is not an author of confusion but of peace. Now follow me

[He leads them out side to a waiting van]

This van will take you to the city. Once you are outside you can then decide what to do with yourself. But if I may advice you just report to American embassy to arrange for your flight home.

Johnny

[Forces a smile]

Thanks all the same. I don't think our going home will solve the problem.

[Shakes his hand].

One other thing Father our wisdom, education, doctrine or what ever we posses can not dictate the pattern by which God intervenes in human affairs, every thing works for good for them that love God

[They look at each other for a very long time]

Thanks for everything—

{They shake hands again before they enter the van]

Please take us to the nearest police station.

SCENE 22

Outside[Chief Adaka's compound is the Chief, his two wives three members of his cabinet and two other bodyguards]

Chief Adaka
[Raising his voice when he sees them approaching]

Akilika where did you find him.

Akilika
[Whispering into his ear]

Where did I find you, in the girl's house?

Chief
[This time very angry]

Akilika! I am talking to you! Where did you find him?

Nze. Okeke
[Comes in at this time]

Chief we should first of all chase the fox away before we blame the chickens for wondering far into the bush. Your son is back safely that is all that matters. You are the Chief of the land and he is free to go anywhere he chooses to go. Our main concern now is the white man and his wife. If anything happens to them the government will hold you responsible. And your enemies will rejoice over it.

Chief Adaka

Yes My Enemies. If they can not get me they look for my son. Who else is seeking for my downfall, Nze Aka Anu and his Ogbondu council of elders. They are now using the name of Ogbondu to seek my downfall.

Nze Ikenna

[Interrupting]

The Chief Priest and his group were not at the Village Square when the people gathered. The fact is that the people mobilized themselves and went on rampage. It was the village town criers that summoned the people to the Village Square.

Nze Okeke—

Somebody must have given the town criers the order to summon the people. Now if I may ask you is it possible for anyone in Edeani to summon the people without the Chief's knowledge.

Nze Ikenna

[Stressing his point with his walking stick]

Who summoned them is not the issue, the issue remains clear something happened that triggered the anger of the people.

First for the first time in the history of Edeani the authority of Ogbondu is challenged. Secondly Okwuonu refused to give his daughter out to the service of Ogbondu in accordance to our custom. Thereby creating a new dangerous precedent for people to disobey our custom and tradition and run to the outcast religion.

Thirdly to add insult to injury the white man and his church killed the sacred snake.

Finally I am now a living witness that your son has started to develop a relationship with Ogbondu's bride. Which you know is an abomination.

Chief Adaka—

[Very surprised]

Now you are coming. I like to see my enemies out of their closet. Stop hiding! Come out! Nze Okeke you are very right we should first of all chase the fox before we blame the chickens. This incident will expose all my enemies one after the other. Ikenna when the time comes you will explain in details who mobilized the people to trace my son to the church. Secondly find the whereabouts of the white man and his wife and finally you name those responsible for the burning down of the church and people's home. I believe you know very much about this incident.

Nze Okeke

[Trying to calm him down]

It is okay I don't think Ikenna intends to personalize this issue but to give an insight into certain areas of our custom and tradition we tend to ignore at this critical time. I would advise every one of us to go home and rest. It is already late. By tomorrow I strongly believe the white man and his wife will be found. The search parties are out looking for them. Chief, please let us suspend this discussion. The chief's cabinet and the council of elders will meet to handle the issue. We are all members of this group.

Chief Adaka

Nze Okeke I have always respected your opinion on many vital issues. I don't think there is any need for such a meeting now because the accused can not be the judge. The constitution of this land rests on me the custodian of custom and tradition of Edeani.

[As he was saying this he starts to move towards the gate that leads to his house but suddenly he seems to have remembered something very important and turns back]

That reminds me, you said something about my son going after the Ogbondu's wife. Why didn't the chief priest and his clique recommend any of your daughters? Why I say why? You have five grown up girls why go to a poor farmer with only a child. Tell me why.

Nze Ikenna—

Ogbondu makes his selection or does the same constitution gives you power over the gods of the land.

Chief Adaka

I tell you why

[He goes straight to where Lynda is standing with Ebuka's sister and gently pulls her towards himself]

Because your daughters are not as beautiful as she is. Look at her stop crying my dear. Smile my dear and show them how beautiful you are.

[Members of chief's household are forced to laugh even Lynda forces a smile]

Now Obidia

[He beckons to his first wife]

Please take good care of her for the night.

[To members of his household]

Now everybody go inside

[To the elders].

You can tell a blind man that there is no oil in the food he eats but you can not tell him there is no salt. We are all elders of this land. when the god makes a mistake somebody must suffer. We know every thing going on in that shrine and who decides for the gods. Good night.

[He goes inside and as they are moving, Akilika pulls Ebuka by his shirt]

Akilika

Whispering into his ears]

Didn't I tell you he is a god of his own. Now the goods are delivered to you in good condition.

Ebuka
[Pushing him aside]

Leave me alone crazy man.

SCENE 23

Chief Adaka is having a discussion with the Divisional Police Officer [DPO.] in his office.

Chief Adaka—
[Handing over to him a list of paper]

The people on that list are the ring leaders behind the uprising. They should be arrested.

DPO
[Still looking at the list on the table and lightening his cigarette]

. Well! Well! No problem let us say 2000 naira for each person therefore, for 10 Let just say 20000naira. Well it is a deal. This evening, my men will storm the village and arrest them all. Is that okay with you.

Chief Adaka
[Looking left and right and lowering his voice]

How much do I get out of it?

DPO—
It is left for you All we ask is 2000naira for each person. You are the Chief.

Chief

[Forcing a smile]

That is okay. One other thing I want the arrest to be made very early in the morning our customs forbids elders from sleeping outside the village against their will. That will give the town union enough time to collect the money before nightfall.

DPO

-*[At this stage the intercom on the DPO table rings. He picks it up and listens]*

Then bring them in, Chief you are lucky the white MAN and his WIFE are already here

.*[There is a tap on the door as a police officer ushers them in and leaves]*

You may sit down. This is chief Adaka. You should have know him'

Chief

That means things have turned upside down I am supposed to introduce you to the DPO and not the other way round.

Johnny

We have been trying to make out time to pay a visit to the palace before this incident happened. I am really sorry. Your son I learnt was in the church and saw every thing that happened.

Chief

Yes and that is why I am here to make sure the organizers of this evil are dealt with.

Mary

I hope no lives were lost?

Chief

None to the best of my knowledge

[*Standing up this time*]

I have made a formal report therefore no need for another. Let us go. You can stay in my palace for now.

DPO

{*Spreading his hand*]

He is the eye of the government in this village. You can go with him if there is any more problem, just let me know

. [*They all shake hands and leave*].

SCENE 24

In the debris of their burnt home Mazi Okwuonu sits with his wife who is weeping.

Mazi Okwuonu

I have told you to stop destroying yourself for nothing because I know our daughter is alive. I saw the young man move with her through the window.

Lynda's Mother—
If she is alive where is she

[*Speaking in tears*]

Where is she, this is the second day.

[*She kneels down in tears and raises her hands towards the sky*]

Oh Jesus it is because of you she has refused to obey the law of the land. If you are really what she claims you are let me see her alive again I promise to join her in serving you I will worship you all my life.

[*It is at this stage Ebuka rides in with her into the compound*]

Mazi Okwuonu
[*Mazi is the first to see them coming*].

Now this is your daughter.

[*Ebuka parks his bicycle a short distance from where they are and walks with Lynda towards them.*]

Lynda's Mother
[*With tears of joy she jumps from her seat to embrace her daughter and later Ebuka also*]

Oh my God so you are alive

[*She holds her tight to her self and later she turns to Ebuka*]

Thank you my son for going after her in the midst of that confusion. At least you have saved her from those criminals.

Mazi Okwuonu—
[*Still shaking hands with Ebuka*]

Thank you my son come and sit down

. [*Pointing at a cane chair*]

You can see the damage these hoodlums have done to my house. Now tell me what happened. In our own case my wife and I had no alternative than to run to my in law's village. It was really a difficult decision for my wife especially without her daughter. The following day my in—law restrains us from coming. They felt it was not safe for us to do so considering the fact that our family might be the target of the attacks. This morning we decided to come and face whatever consequence.

Ebuka
Even my father was very disturbed. He made it clear to us he has nothing to do with it. He was the one who advised her not to leave the palace until a formal report was made to the police. I came here yesterday morning but saw no one.

[It is at this stage they start to hear noises coming from the next compound of people wailing, weeping and shouting. They all get up and start to move towards the scene.

SCENE 25

Two vans loaded with policemen and a Black Maria storm the next compound to complete the arrest of the 10ᵗʰ elder in the village Nze Ikenna. There is weeping, wailing and shouting as villagers follow the van from compound to compound as the arrest is been made.

The police shoot a gun into the air to disperse the crowd before they gently take the old man to join others already in the van. After this they fire more gun shuts and drive off while the crowd wail and continued to shout.

SCENE 26

At the palace reception hall sit elders of the village and the town union executives having a very serious debate.

Chief Adaka

[Presiding]

Now when a man is in a hurry and breaks the yam tuber, he must sit down to find the remains. I Adaka Ogwumagana was not informed when the town criers summoned the people, nor was I informed when the people went on rampage. Now the 10 elders who master minded the whole thing are in the hands of the government then Adaka Ogwumagana was remembered. Okay what do you people want me to do?.

Nze Okeke
[*Pays tribute to the chief and the elders around*]

My question goes to the town criers I really want to know who asked you people to call the assembly of the villagers when even chief Adaka claims before us now he is not aware of that.

Amabo Crier
I heard the voice of Okoro Udenwa of Umuota village making the cries then I took my gong and joined him. You all know I have been out of the village for sometimes now I happened to be back that very day. When I had him I thought may be the chief and the elders are fully aware of it.

First Villager
You are a liar Okoro Udenwa has been in hospital for the past two weeks.

[*Others claim the chief priest gave the order. Others shouted them down*]

Second Villager
Shut up all of you. The Chief priest of Ogbondu has nothing to do with it

Town Union President
[*Shouting at the top of his voice*]

I want every person to listen. We have spent hours in this place discussing only one issue who summoned the people. If I may ask is that the issue at stake now? The issue at stake now is that 10 elders of our community are in police net how do we raise money to bail them out before nightfall. We all know it is an abomination for the elders to sleep outside the village against their wish. Now Chief Adaka you are the eye of the government in this community how much will it take us to bail these elders before nightfall.

Chief Adaka

[*Clears his voice*]

Bailing them today is not the issue, if we can raise 3000naira for each of them we will have them before nightfall. The issue is who will sign the bail bond on the following government conditions, that they will—:

[1] Rebuild the church
[2] Rebuild the missionary's home
[3] Rebuild people' burnt down homes
[4] Pay compensation for the properties destroyed
[5] Guaranty the safety of life and property of the white man and his wife.

The government views the actions of these people as criminals and unconstitutional. To them every person is free to worship any god he likes. This gathering must agree on that before we talk of bailing them out.

Okay Ikenna

If we agree on these terms who then compensates us on the death of Ogbondu snake. We all know our tradition demands for a befitting funeral to be financed only by one who caused its death. I know the same constitution our chief has just quoted for us recognizes the people's tradition and customs. These 10 elders who include my own father are defending the custom and tradition of Edeani. It will be a great shame if they spend a night outside this village against their wish. From what the chief is telling us now we have to compensate the white man and the church for killing the sacred snake but he fails to tell us who pays for the funeral of the sacred snake as custom demands. Who will compensate us on the loss of our cherished Ogbondu. Every one of you present will agree with me that things will never be the same again Ogbondu is the nucleus that binds us together and today that cord is broken. It is now every man to his family. Chief Adaka I am sorry to say this, your mission seems to have been accomplished. It has been your desire since you were appointed the warrant chief of Edeani to destroy the custom and tradition of this village. My father and these elders now in police net have always stood against it.

[This time, many supporters of chief shout him down while others want him to continue. The whole place becomes rowdy. Chief's bodyguards try in vain to calm people down. At this stage Chief leaves through the back door.

SCENE 27

At the home of Aka Dike the greatest native doctor in Edeani and beyond is. Chief Adaka.

Chief Adaka
[Presenting to him some silver coins and a live cock]

Our elders say a toad does not run in the afternoon for nothing. You are a personal friend to my father. I have always depended on your power and it has never failed me. Now something is wrong somewhere. Some groups of people are after my throne.

Doctor
[*Clears his throat and smiles*]—

Chief Adaka Ogwumagana anyone who fights you is my enemy. Your father and I were under oath. But I will not join you to fight against the gods. You have given sanctuary to the greatest enemy of the land and have closed your eyes to your son's relationship with Ogbondu's maiden. The gods wants to come after you but I have made sacrifices on your behalf. Now you must drop 25 pieces of silver coins to enable me make consultation with the spirit world.

[*Chief dips his hands into his pocket and brings the coins which he drops on the floor. Aka Dike counts them to make sure they are correct before entering a small door at the side of his alter. Inside this room he uncovers a mirror hidden behind a black cloth on the wall. He starts to make incantations. As he is speaking there come a noise like a rushing wind and suddenly in the midst of this noise one like the prince of mermaid appears in the mirror full of smiles.*]

The Prince
Aka Dike you have done well. Now tell him I am very angry with him but that you have pleaded on his behalf.

Tell him that I can only be appeased through a special sacrifice.

[*This time he starts to speak in a strange tong which Aka Dike seems to understand because he nods his head in response to what he says.*]

[*Outside the room Chief Adaka sits and waits while his mind goes to a time when he came to the same doctor for charms. Using special effect system he is shown lying on a bamboo bed with stones as a cover. His body covered with blood from tiny razor cuts inflicted on him by the native doctor. The native doctor is also seen rubbing charm all over his body. Chief Adaka is seen gyrating like a wounded snake.*

Native Doctor

No man born of a woman will ever harm you and after this any one who wants to kill you must first of all destroy his or her self.

[*He becomes awake from his little dream when Aka Dike comes out from the room*]

Native Doctor

Adaka Ogwumagana the gods are really angry with you but with me you have no problem. You are now going to make a covenant with the gods. After this all your enemies will bow before you.

[*He places a small coffin on the floor and lights up candles of different colors round about it. In this coffin comes out smoke from burning incense. He brings out two objects like kola nuts he chews one and gives one to Chief to do the same, which he does. After which he makes a cut on chief's finger and allows the blood to drop into the coffin. As this is done the smoke intensifies. Chief stands like a lifeless object. Using special effects his spirit is seen leaving the body.*

SCENE 28 SPIRIT WORLD

The prince of Ogbondu is seen walking up and down like a frustrated man and one after the other his agents sneak in and sit down in fears around him.

The Prince
[*Looks at them one after the other*]

Fear! Fear! I can see fear in your faces. It is too late to fear. Our time is running out.

He starts to undergo transformation into different forms and objects from young man to a very old man].

Fear means early death. If we are cast out of this territory where do we go?

[*This time he changes back to the prince*]

We must fight to finish.

[*He starts to speak in tongues. Suddenly the spirit of Chief Adaka walks into the palace. All the little agents go to a corner in fear. The prince joins himself with the spirit of*

Chief and they become one. He then turns into a very big bat and flies away.

SCENE 29

AT OGBONDU SHRINE
Aka Dike the native doctor is seen presiding over this meeting.

Aka Dike

An elder does not stay in a house and watch a goat die in child birth. I am guided by the spirits to call this meeting of unity. For peace to reign there must be the willingness to sacrifice. For without sacrifice there will be no reconciliation. I am happy to see you elders back. I want every one of you to see your ordeal as personal sacrifice for the peace in Edeani. Chief Adaka himself has sworn an oath before the gods of this land to work with you elders for the progress of this village. But before I perform the reconciliation rituals we must reach an agreement.

[From his bag he brings out bamboo sticks cut into same sizes which he gives some to each member. In front of them is a calabash full of blood.

[1] This committee will stand as the supreme authority of the land.
[2] Any one going contrary to its decision attracts the wrath of the gods.
[3] The burial ceremony of the sacred snake must be financed by the white man.

[4] Chief Adaka is recognized as the mouthpiece of this group in Edeani. Any decision taken by this group must reach the people through him.

[5] Mazi Okwuonu must send his daughter to the shrine according to tradition.

[6] Finally this committee must always stand as one to challenge any one or group that tries to disobey its decision.

[As each agreement is mentioned each member drops a stick into the calabash. After which they take a kola nut from another calabash, dips into the one full of blood and eat. A ram is roasted and they eat together.

SCENE 30

Johnny, Mary, Ebenizer and two elders of the church sit in a closed door meeting with Chief, Ogbondu high priest and two other elders.

Chief Adaka

I will start by blaming you the elders of the church. You people tried to operate in this village without consulting us the elders of the land. At least I am the warrant chief of this land I represent the interest of every group in this community. Presently I have signed an agreement with the police to create a good atmosphere for you to perform your mission in this village. Also after the release of the elders we have come together in agreement for the interest of peace and to join forces as you can see to ensure that the last incident does not occur again. Now we need your own contribution to help bring peace in this community.

Therefore we have agreed as follows—:

[1] The church should finance the funeral of the sacred snake.

[2] That the girl Lynda should spend a full market week in the shrine to prepare her for the final hand over to the shrine

[3] That the church should not interfere with the custom and tradition of the people while we give you the assurance that the people will not interfere with your activity. Finally we also promise to help rebuild the church and the missionary's house that is the much we can do for now.

[*He turns to the elders*]

I hope I have said it all?

[*The elders nod in agreement*]

Johnny
[*Shocked and surprised*]

I thank you all for coming together in trying to bring peace in the village. I promise that the church will do every thing possible within its power to contribute in doing the same.—Based on what you've just said it is not possible to mix spiritual things with physical things.

[*Pointing at the chief priest*]

You were at the shrine and saw what really happened. Have you ever sat down to ask yourself what powers were behind the death of the sacred snake or do you still believe any man could have killed such a big snake with his hand. You are all elders tell your children the truth. We are not going to quarrel over this issue, that same power that killed the snake kept me here and the same power will protect the church and its members. Secondly I did not come here by my own power, God almighty directed me from America to come and be the instrument he will use to set you people free. Free from slavery, poverty and blindness.

High Priest—

[*Quick to reply*]

What do you mean? That we are slaves, poor and blind.

Johnny

What you believe and do shows what you are. First the snake you worship as god died at the name of Jesus. And you still believe it has powers over you. Why not believe and accept the truth. Neither you nor I can change the truth. If the snake is god then the god is dead. The truth remains that as elders you should look for another god.

Chief Adaka

We have not come to argue with you but to give instructions. There are two alternatives to this and one must be followed. It is either you bow down to the demands of the people or you leave this village before four market weeks. I have done all I could for you. After this period of grace I will make a formal report to the police that I can not guarantee your safety in this village.

[With that statement they leave]

Ebenezer

The situation is becoming very tricky. It seems the two groups have come together against us. Chief Adaka is very unpredictable. He can do any thing to destroy our mission. He might even bribe the police to support his fight against us. The only option we have is either—:

[1] To give them money to perform the ceremony or—

[2] We trust God and say no to all their demands. It is up to you to decide.

Johnny—

What is your own opinion?

Ebenezer

For me and my people we have nothing to lose in fighting on, because the people regard us as outcast and nothing can change that from their mind. Our main concern is you and your wife. It is only in Christ we have freedom. You don't really know what it means to be regarded as an outcast and untouchable by people you see every day as your own people. Your children can not marry whom they choose or be married to whom they like. You are worst than a leper, some how fighting on and dying for it is more preferably than living a life in which your generation yet unborn have no class. You may not understand but what ever you say is okay for us.

Johnny

[There is silence for sometime]

I want you to know from today that they are the people who are in bondage. The word of God says in—:

> *Voice—Romans 8:1 There is therefore now no condemnation to them which are in Christ Jesus, who walk not after the flesh, but after the spirit.*

They are in a more terrible bondage. Your own experience though painful is a physical bondage that ends with this world system. But theirs is a more terrible bondage that might end in hell fire. Now God is using you and I to set them free from Satan and his agents. I want you all to know that this battle is not between us and the Chief or these elders but with that evil spirit who calls himself Ogbondu. He is the same spirit I saw in Loss Angeles, the same spirit my wife saw in her office computer. Like what happened in the bible two big time enemies Pontius Pilate and Herod settled their differences just to condemn and crucify the lord Jesus. Today the same has happened before us. The Chief who some time ego master minded the arrest of these elders has joined forces with them to drive us away and stop the work of God. Well, it is not by power, nor by might, but by my spirit says the Lord. Let us pray.

SCENE 31

In the room Johnny and his wife are sleeping. Mary is awake. She sits on the only cane chair opposite the bed. It is at this stage the agent of darkness comes in and starts to speak into her thought

[Using special effect this ugly demon will be shown talking to her.

> *Voice—Don't allow your husband to undo what God has done for you. The stage is now set for every member of this community to become Christians. The snake is dead, the chief and the elders have promised to build the church and your house for you. All they need from you is to help them save face before the people. You don't need to participate in the ceremony. All you need is to give them the money not even all just some. The chief will complete the rest. Don't allow your husband to insist. They will chase you out and the church members will suffer more. After all the bible says give unto Caesar what is to Caesar and to God what is to God. Even St Paul agrees with this when he said in 1 Corinthians 9:20—*

> *Voice—And unto Jews I became as a Jew, that I might gain the Jews, to them that are under the law, as under the law, that I might gain them that are under the law. Why not yield to their demand and gain them for Christ.*

[This time Johnny wakes up and is surprised to see her sitting on the chair].

Johnny—

What is wrong? You are not sleeping? I hope you are not having a nightmare.

Mary—

The spirit of God has just spoken to me. I am led by the spirit to read the word of God.

Voice—1 Cor. 9:20

My dear I think we should give them the money. I don't really believe it amount to compromising our faith or that we believe in their god. We are only being obedient to the word of God. I am really disturbed. We have no where to go. Already we are in his house, we eat his food, he shelter's us and finally he is rebuilding the church for us. We need to show a little appreciation.

Johnny

Wait a minute you mean giving money to perform the funeral of a dead god does not mean compromising our faith. Oh my God! Are you still a baby in this race?

Okay, how about the poor girl Lynda? Are we to give her up to the shrine? She will be their next demand. Tell me should we give her up?.

Mary

I know it, since we came here I have been finding it difficult to understand your mind. I am no more in the picture you don't even regard my opinion any more. I am like no body in this mission. You only come to me when you are pressed. You are now a powerful man of God. No one else hears from God

[She starts to weep Johnny goes to her and tries to console her]

Leave me alone

If I am no more useful to the mission here please send me to the states.

[At this stage she breaks down and starts to cry and falls into his arm. This time there is a knocking at the door].

Johnny

Yes? Who is that? Come in the door is open.

.[The door opens and chief Adaka comes in. As he is entering Johnny sees in a moment the picture of the prince of mermaid reflected in his face and disappearing immediately]

Chief

[Smiling]

I am sorry to disturb you

[Seems to notice her crying]

My daughter, I hope he has not given you overdose. White man I tell you one secret about black men. Do you know why black men beat up their wives in the middle of the night

[Johnny and wife sit down amazed but still looking at him with interest].

Johnny

No I want to know.

Chief

Because women seems to be more romantic when they cry. All you need to do is to pet her, wipe her tears, lay her down gently. Well you know the rest.

Johnny

Are you saying that is what I am doing now?

Chief

[Pointing to Mary]

Did he do that?

[This time they all start to laugh including Mary]

Now my friend you can see I really want this issue to end amicably. All you need is to give something no matter how small. I will call the elders and this issue will end the following day. It doesn't mean you should bear the whole thing. I am always your friend.

Johnny

Chief the issue is not as simple as you make it out to be. This is more complex and more deadly. Your own life is at stake, your wives, your children and every member of this community. We are dealing with an evil spirit. Whose mission is to [1] Steal, [2] Kill and [3] Destroy

God's purpose in this village. Forget what name you call him Ogbondu or what ever. I have seen him with my own eyes far away in the states. He is the agent of Satan representing him in this territory. We need to cast him out and not to appease him—So that the glorious light of our Lord Jesus will shine in this village.

Chief

[*Very surprised*]

You are taking the whole thing too far. I don't really see what the funeral ceremony of the sacred snake got to do with the spirit you saw in your dream or even the one your wife saw in her office.

Johnny

[*Looks very shocked and alarmed*]

Chief how did you come to know about my dream and that of my wife.

[*This time he gets up shaking his head like some one going crazy. This time he starts to move towards the door. Mary also sees the same vision reflected in his face as he stands by the door*].

Chief

Did I say that? Well you have only four market days to comply.

[*With that statement he leaves them*].

Mary

[*Holds the husband very tightly. She looks very frightened*]

My dear did you notice any thing about his face?

Johnny

Like what?.

Mary

Like the same spirit I saw in my office computer. Oh my God I hope am not going crazy.

Johnny

You are not I saw it the first time he came in.

Mary

Oh my God, did you?

[*Looking straight into his eyes*]

Lets leave here! He is an agent. They may try to destroy us.

[*She starts to weep*]

Let us leave this place.

Johnny

What exactly are you saying? Where on earth do you want us to go tonight, where do you stand? Short time ago you wanted us to compromise with them. Now you want us to run away. Please my dear this is that time the word of God says that the just shall live by faith and not by sight. Encourage yourself with the word of God. Though I walk through the valley of the shadow of death I shall fear no evil. The battle is not ours.—Let us pray

[*They hold each other and start to pray*]

SCENE 32

Lynda is washing clothes outside the make shift hut they have just built. Then suddenly a piece of white paper wrapped in stone falls in front of her. She picks it up, unwraps it and reads the content.

She immediately cleans her hands, looks left and right before going into a nearby bush. She comes to a very big fallen tree and sees Ebuka sitting on a tree trunk.

Lynda—

Ebuka why not leave me alone. Why do you want to destroy yourself? Please Ebuka you are putting yourself into serious danger

Ebuka

This time he comes nearer takes her by the arm and brings her to sit with him at the tree trunk. They look at each other for some time.

Tell me the truth Lynda. Do you think you are the property of Ogbondu

[*They look at each other for a very long time. This time tears start to roll down her cheeks*]

Lynda

Does it matter what I feel. My feelings will not change the situation. It did not stop them burning down the church and my father's house. What I feel now will neither change the situation. Who am I to try and change the situation? Ebuka I am concerned about you because you are exposing yourself to so much danger by coming to me. Ogbondu is not a man but an evil spirit. You may hide your self from the villagers but you can not hide from these evil spirits. They may try to harm you as a warning to others. I don't think you really understand what am saying.

Ebuka

[Making her come nearer to him on the tree trunk]

Sit down! I understand more than you can imagine. Since that vigil I have been disturbed by what the white man said about Christ. In the first place as my mind keeps telling me, America is a dream land of every young man in this country and here is a young educated man with his beautiful wife in this remote village just because God spoke to them. Since that day till now I have not stopped in reading the word of God to know more about Christ. I am now convinced that Christ is the way to abundance life.

[He looks at her again]

I think am in love with you. I want you to promise me one thing that you will never give yourself to Ogbondu shrine.

[*They look at each other it is at this stage they heard Linda's mother calling. She gets up*]

Linda
[*She looks at him tears rolling down her face*]

Ebuka do you really believe Christ as your Lord

[*Ebuka nods his head*] and that he is able to do anything

[*Ebuka nods again*]

Then tell him what you've just told me

[*this time the mother calls again*]

Tell him you love me. Tell Jesus that you love me. I promise I will never go to the shrine.

[*with that statement she leaves*].

SCENE 33

At the church reconstruction site the whole village seems to be there both male and female, old and young. After the work they are all seated to eat the food prepared for them by the church. At the end of the meal Johnny takes his time with Ebenezer his interpreter to give a word of thanks.

Johnny

On behalf of my wife and every member of this church I would like to use this opportunity to thank every one of you for coming to help us rebuild this church. I also want you all to extend my greetings to the chief and other members of his council of elders. They have really matched their word with action. This God we serve will surely bless you all according to his word in—:

Voice—Mathew 10:42—

And whosoever shall give these little ones a cup of cold water only in the name of disciple, verily I say unto you he shall in no wise loose his reward.—

Before we leave this place and you all go to your different houses I want you all to bear in mind that God loves the people of Edeani. That he has to force me and my wife even against our own will to leave America to come here and be a channel of his visitation to you. God wants me to tell the people of Edeani today that there is a thief amongst you. This thief has three missions—: [1] to steal [2] to kill and[3] to destroy God's good plan for you. You may begin to ask me who this thief is. Well the thief is within you. It will be very difficult for you to see him with your naked eyes. I am going to describe some fruits he is bearing amongst you—So that you will be able to identify him. Let us read—;

Voice—Genesis 1:29—30—And God said, behold, I have given you every herb bearing seed, which is upon the face of all the earth and every tree, in the which is the fruit of tree yielding seed to you it

> *shall be for meat. And to every beast of the earth and to every fowl of the air and to every thing that creepeth upon the earth wherein there is life. I have given every green herb for meat and it was so.*

But today this thief I am talking about has forced you people to bow down and worship a snake which if found in the neighboring village becomes food. This same thief has deceived you people to worship objects made by man. I want you all to see what god is saying about that—:

> *Voice—Psalm 115:4—7—Their idols are silver and gold the works of men's hand. They've mouths but they speak not, eyes have they but they see not. They have ears but they hear not nose have they but they smell not: They have hands but they handle not: feet have they but they walk not, neither speak they through their throat—They that make them are like unto them.*

This is the word of God not mine. Now I want us to consider this, what really happened to that sacred snake that very day? Any one who thinks I killed the snake through my own power is just deceiving himself. The truth of this matter can only be found in the word of God—

Voice—Philippians 2:10 that at name of Jesus every knee should bow of things in earth and things under the earth.

Yes that was exactly what happened on that day. I mentioned the name of Jesus. Just when the snake attacked me and you saw what happened. Do you still want to worship a dead God or do you want to worship a living God. Today might be the only chance you have. Now He is knocking at the door of your heart if you open the door he will come in and dine with you. Do not harden your heart just believe this gospel and be free. Let us pray.[He starts a song]

> *It is going to be great today*
> *Thy Holy Ghost is already here*
> *Jesus Christ is already here.*

Suddenly before he can finish the song there comes a sound from no where like a rushing mighty wind, and fills the air and the whole villagers present start to speak in strange tongues.

SCENE 34

IN THE SPIRIT WORLD
The prince of Ogbondu is surrounded by his agents in the palace—:

The Prince
[Looking very angry and terrible]

The Prophecy! In my own territory? And in my own face.

[*With special effect these evil spirits are able to see the villagers under the influence of God's power while at the same time the voice relays to them the prophecy on—*:

> *Voice—Joel 2:28—And it shall come to pass afterwards that I will pour out my spirit upon all flesh and your sons and your daughters shall prophesy, your old men shall dream dreams, your young men shall see visions.*

Why here! I say why? These people belong to us. What does this bastard have to do with these helpless people, I say leave them for me! They are mine. All my field agents have left their post.

[*As he is speaking some of these agents are seen flying into the palace in the form of bats. As they fly in they all gather themselves at a corner in fright*]

As long as this girl has defied my order and still moves freely things can not be the same. These people need a good lesson from me

[*Turning to his agents*]

Now I want all of you to listen. If we loose our control on this people you and I will be going to the pit.

[*In a very angry tone*]

I don't want to go down there now. We must fight to finish. I repeat we must fight to finish. Now come all of you come and see

[*He leads them to unveil a screen on the wall. In it they see demons and other human souls wailing and weeping in hell fire*]

Do you want to go in there before the appointed time? I say do you want to go in now. No territorial kingdom will accept us if we loose our kingdom. Out! All of you out I say.

[*This time he starts to kick them one after the other. They all start to turn into bats one after the other*].

SCENE 35

Chief, Ebuka and Ebuka's mother [Obidia] are seen in serious discussion.

Chief Adaka

Now Obidia you are my first wife and Ebuka is our first son. It will be dangerous for us to close our eyes when we see him going the wrong way. If anything bad happens to him we are going to be held responsible. Now the elders have announced the day of the Ogbondu moonlight ceremony.

[*This announcement seems to shock Obidia most*]

Yes that particular girl that slept with you is the new bride. The gods have spoken and there is nothing we can do about it. That is the main reason why I called you people. Aka Dike the greatest native doctor once told me to remove the monkey's hand from the soup pot before it turns out to become human hands.

[Turning to Ebuka]

I have received several reports about your relationship with this girl. From now on if you have anything to do with her cut it off. She is the property of Ogbondu. I am your father and I am ready to stand by you at any time but not against the gods of the land. I hope I have made myself clear. Have nothing to do with her, further contact with her will attract the anger of the gods in this family. Obidia, talk to your son, this will be my last warning on this issue. You know the implication of such a relationship. The date of her wedding will be announced after tonight's ceremony.

Obidia

[Looks very surprise]

You mean the moonlight ceremony will be held against her wish is that the new law

[She starts to nod her head]

So the rumor is true.

Chief Adaka—

What rumor?

Obidia

That the God of the outcast people has destroyed Ogbondu and that Ogbondu has left Edeani.

Chief

Who is spreading that nonsense?

Obidia

Then why not leave Ogbondu to take action against any disobedience as it use to be. Why force the poor girl?. Well that is not the issue Ebuka is not a child anymore. You should ask him what kind of relationship he is having with her, apart from rescuing her from the hands of the villagers.

Chief

Does it matter?. He is young and might be attracted to her beauty. It is our duty to warn him before it becomes too dangerous.

Obidia

Just like every other man might be attracted to her even adults like you and the so-called elders. After all Ogbondu is a spirit he is not the one that breeds babies for these women betrothed to it.

[At this stage Ebuka starts to laugh]

Chief

You see so you are in full support of him. You are inviting the anger of the gods into my compound. I will not tolerate that from you any more or you leave this compound for me.

Ebuka

[Full of anger]

She can not leave this compound. I mean she deserves to be spoken to with more respect and not every time I will send you home. She is too old for that. Enough is enough.

Yes I am a grown up person and I have every right to my own feelings even towards any person Ogbondu or no Ogbondu.

Chief

[*Very surprised*]

Is that so! So you've started your law practice with me. Well not so bad I paid for it. What ever your feelings are that girl becomes untouchable after tonight's ceremony. Is that clear any contact with her attracts the anger of the gods.

[*He leaves them after that statement*]

Obidia

[*Turning to her son*]

You have heard him what have you got to say?

Ebuka

[*Very calm*]

Mother I think God has reserved that girl for me. I know it and I believe it.

Obidia

[*Very surprised*]

Oh my God what have you done with her?

Ebuka

Nothing Mum. I just know I love her.

222

Obidia

[Silent for a while]

Have you told her or let her know about it?

Ebuka

We don't need to say it we just feel it when ever we are together. Why do you ask?

Obidia

[looking very exhausted]

Oh my God what is happening? I must tell you too since that night she slept with us in this house, I have always seen her guiding me around this compound in my old age. What is really happening? And tonight your father and their evil clique are going to force her into the shrine for that devilish ceremony. Oh I pity the poor girl, such a piece of beauty. How can I help her. My mind tells me always that she belongs to this palace. Please if you can avoid her because they will destroy you.

[she weeps silently]

All they want is to defile her and drop her where they have dropped others. I hope that God she worships will save her now.

Ebuka

[Standing up]

Mom do you mean they are going to bundle her like a goat to the shrine. No way Not as long as I am alive.

[He goes straight to where he parked his bike and rides off]

SCENE 36

Lynda is alone in her room reading the bible. She drops the bible and drifts into a dream. In her dream she finds herself in Ebuka's arm. He holds her tightly to himself and some how she manages to look into his face. He smiles at her.

Lynda
Ebus—Will you let them take me away from you.

Ebuka
It will be over my dead body.

[He bends down to kiss her when suddenly knocking on the door wakes her up. She gets up and opens the door for Ebuka who seems to be in a hurry.

Lynda
Ebuka what is wrong?

Ebuka
Come with me. They are coming to take you by force to the shrine tonight. Come let us go

[Almost dragging her by force]

Lynda
Where are we going my parents are not around.

[She becomes confused]

Ebuka
Forget about them now lets get out of here

.*[He takes her to his bicycle and they ride off]*.

SCENE 37

Chief and some members of the council of elders are seen entering his compound.

Chief Adaka
[looks very angry and almost shouting]

Obidia! Obidia!

-*[This time Ebuka's mother comes out from her room]*

Where is Ebuka and the girl.

Obidia—
[Looks confused]

Am I supposed to follow them wherever they go. What is wrong?

Chief

Are you asking me what is wrong? My question is where are they? People saw him this night with the girl. You and your son want to bring the anger of the gods into this family. If you know where they are you better tell us now.

Obidia

I don't know. Even if I know can any one fight for the gods.

Nze Okeke

Em Obidia. Wait a minute!. Do you really know the girl in question. The issue at stake now is not a family matter. It is an issue that deals with Ogbondu shrine. You are a respected woman in this village you know the implication of what we are talking. Tonight is the bridal moonlight ceremony at the shrine and your son is said to have fled with a bride betrothed to the gods. You know the consequence of his action. Please if you know their where about tell us now.

Obidia

I don't know. That is exactly what I have just said.

Chief Adaka

[*Very furious and at the same time pointing his walking stick at her*]

That evil you are trying to invite into this compound surely will come upon you.

At this moment he feels a pang of pain in his chest and stomach. He starts to slump, they are all amazed and confused. Before they can really get the picture of what is going on he has fallen down. Obidia starts to shout. While the elders join hand to sit him up. This time members of chief's household gather. There are weeping and wailing.

SCENE 38

At the temporary home still under construction by the villagers sit Johnny his wife, Ebenezer, Ebuka and Lynda.

Johnny—
Bro. Ebenezer can you please shed more light on the subject concerning this moon light ceremony?

Ebenezer
So many stories have been told about what goes on in that ceremony. It is like the bachelor's eve. The lady is free to enjoy herself and meet with her human friends before going into final marriage with the gods. It is only the members of the Ogbondu council of elders can give an authentic account of what goes on there. The victims themselves can not tell because they remain in a trance throughout the ceremony. So many claims are made ranging from [1] Group sex [2] Vaginal mutilation [3] Bestiality and [4] Finally some claim something is taken from the victim's body to prepare charms. Whichever one is true after this ceremony the victim automatically becomes an outcast or untouchable so is their offspring's. To me the whole thing is demonic and I personally advise her not to go near the shrine.

Johnny
[In a very serious note]

That last statement of yours is what I want us to follow. Now listen every one of you my mind is telling me that we have reached the climax of our mission in this village. The battle is not between any one of us here. Not even with the chief and his council of elders. My mind tells me that the territorial spirit of this area knows his time is running out. He is raging a final battle to regain a lost ground. We must not loose hope now. Ogbondu or what ever he is called is fighting to save face in this village. The bible says that anyone entrusted into His hand cannot be taken away.

[*Turning to Lynda*]

Your protection is divinely provided Lynda. You don't need to fear anything. We are going to pray now and hand you over to God including Ebuka who is sticking his life to give help.

Mary

[*Interrupting*]

But if I may ask, Ebuka, why are you risking your life and that of your family in helping her.

Johnny

[*Surprised*]

But why do you ask?

Mary

You can see they are not kids any more as a church we must know if there is anything-special going on between them. I mean any kind of bond or just something.

Johnny

[*Anger written all over his face*]

I really don't see what it got to do with what we are saying now.

Ebenizer

Yes! it means a lot, in whatever action we take, for example if they have agreed to marry or that she is pregnant by him. If they are in any form of agreement like the ones I have just mentioned then his own life is at risk. He is seen as one challenging the gods and must be dealt with.

Johnny

[*Draws his wife nearer to him and kisses her*]

And that was why God calls you my helper. Thanks anyway. So young man, do you have anything to say about this?

Ebuka

Actually I feel Lynda and I are made for each other. To be frank I have not told her but my mother knows everything and she feels the same. She even knows I am going to hide her from these men.

Mary

[*Caressing Lynda's hair*]

Lynda do you love him?—

[*She keeps silent.*]

Loving him anyway does not make you a sinner before God

Lynda
[*She just looks at Ebuka and smiles before covering her face*]

Johnny

[*Starts to laugh*]

This is really complicated. Well one thing I know is that God works in a very mysterious way. Young man the word of God says in psalm 37:4—Delight thyself also in the Lord and he will give thee the desires of thy heart. I will only pray for the will of God to prevail.

Let us pray.

SCENE 39

Ebuka and Lynda are walking at night. As they walk they run into the bush and take cover whenever they hear the noise of people coming from the opposite direction. Just a few poles before they reach the palace they see two elders coming towards them from the palace. They rush into the bush and hide themselves. From where they hide they can here their voices—

Aka Dike
What struck Chief Adaka is a lesson to those who think Ogbondu can not fight for himself. Taking him to the hospital will not even solve his problem.

Chief Priest
Do you mean Ogbondu has started to act.? That will be a lesson to those who are spreading the rumor that Ogbondu is dead.

Aka Dike
It is not even advisable to take any action whatsoever without first consulting the gods. Do you think he is going to survive it.

Chief Priest

I am not sure. That is what that stubborn son of his has brought on him.

[Ebuka and Lynda listen from where they are hiden].

Ebuka.
Oh, my God. It seems something bad has happened to my father. You heard all they said. Come let us go and see.

Lynda
[Tears rolling down her face, she holds Ebuka by the hand and pulls him towards herself]

Ebuka going with you is very dangerous. Please you've exposed yourself and family to danger because of me. You can see what is happening. Your family may not want to see me. Please let me go and see my parents. I will not go with you.

Ebuka
[*Pulling her gently towards himself*]

It is too late for that now we are both in it and we quit the same time. Let's go.

[*They move into the palace through the back to a small door behind the palace building*]

You wait here.

[*He jumps over the fence into the compound and after a short while he opens the small door for Lynda to enter. The compound is empty. They go directly to Ebuka's room*].

Ebuka
Please just feel at home, no one is going to disturb you here. Let me go and see what is going on

.[*This time he holds her to himself*]

I am ready to do anything to protect you Okay?

[*She nods her head*]

He leaves her and goes away

SCENE 40

Lynda's mother is seen weeping, her father, Johnny, Mary and Ebenezer sit in conference.

Mazi Okwuonu

Yes they came here demanding for my daughter that I should release her or face the consequence. In short I was confused, after all I don't even know her whereabouts. Secondly what they are doing has never happened in the history of Edeani for Ogbondu council members to enforce a moonlight ceremony. The fear of punishment from the gods have always led people to obey without question. When I questioned them on that they accused me of so many things—:

[1] Spreading rumors that Ogbondu is dead.
[2] Bewitched Chief Adaka's son into falling in love with my daughter and so many other things I can not remember. Please where is my daughter? Who knows?

Mary
[Still consoling Lynda's mother]

You don't need to worry she is fine and in good shape, that is why we have came to tell you that.

Johnny

Just in case you want to know Chief's son brought her to the church and promised to protect her from been forced to the shrine. For the time been there is nothing we can do because we are part of chief's household.

[At this stage Ada Jeso walks in looking very impatient]

Ada Jeso

The news going on in the village is that an evil force has struck down Chief Adaka. They say he might not survive it.

[This time Lynda's mother starts to weep openly while Mary continues to console her]

Where is Lynda? Please she should be taken to another village this night.

Mary

Why do you say that?

Ada Jeso

Aka Dike the greatest native doctor has just made consultations with the gods and the only hope for the Chief's survival is to bring the girl to the shrine.

Mazi Okwuonu

[He can not control himself he weeps bitterly]

I know she is in that compound. Do you think the chief's household will hide her and see their father dead? No! They will give her out to save the chief. I am going to that house to bring her back. I have sworn over my dead body will they take her to the shrine.

[He goes into his room and brings a machete and a den gun. Johnny and Ebenezer struggle for a long time before they can disarm him].

Johnny

Please Mazi sit down

[This time he sits and starts to weep like a child]

Every thing works for good for them that love God. Mazi you need to have faith and see the power of God.

[This time other members of the church start to arrive]

Now I will want the church to remain in this compound with my wife and in prayer. For God's divine intervention. Ebenezer and myself will be going to the palace to see what we can do.

[Turning to Mazi]

Please stop every action you want to take and just trust God for the first time. Let us pray.

[He starts a song]

Song—Paul and Silas—They prayed—They sang—thy Holy Ghost came down.

SCENE 41

When Ebuka comes, he sees his father lying helplessly on the bed; his eyes wide open, his mouth foaming. His mother is shown soaking water in a towel and cleaning his body.

Ebuka

Oh my God what is wrong with him? Mom, what happened?

[Chief's second wife, Nze Ikenna Akilika, Two other chief's body guard, Okeke, and chief's children were present. There is general weeping and wailing]

Nze Okeke

You are asking what happened. Where is the girl you are hiding?

Ebuka

What has that little girl got to do with this. Mummy! Let us take him to the hospital, Akilika call his driver Mummy we must take him to the hospital.

Nze Okeke

The solution is not with hospital, you are the one that holds the key to his survival. That girl you are hiding belongs to Ogbondu. Obidia speak to your son. You want the blood of chief Adaka in your hands. Remember Ogbondu may not end up in one person. I told you before that this problem is not a family issue. It is bigger than you can imagine. The only thing that will appease the gods is to hand over the girl to the shrine.

[At this time chief starts to struggle like someone under an intensive heat. With the help of Nze Okeke, Obidia pulls of his regalia, by this time Johnny and Ebenezer

are walking into the house while at the same time the spirit of the prince of darkness is leaving chief's body. Immediately this spirit comes out he puts his hand into chief's body and drags his spirit out also. With special effect the two spirits are moving outside the building.

Nze Okeke

Now I want every one of you to listen. I am here because Chief Adaka is my personal friend. You can see that all the elders have gone in a hurry. Why? Because they all saw that the hand of the gods is upon him. Obidia if you and your son can not produce that girl to the elders now I will also join them.

Obidia
[*Very confused and weeping*]

Oh my God. Ebuka! Where is the girl. Please save your father

Second Wife

If my husband dies his blood will be on your head and that of your son.

[*She leaves*]

Akilika
[*Speaking into his ears*]

Where did you hide her.

Johnny

It is okay I don't think that innocent girl has anything to do with chief's sickness. Please let us be calm and see the power of God.

[*He goes to Obidia*]

I want you to believe that, that same God I worship will save your husband. Do you believe?

[*She nods*] [*He then turns to the rest*]

Please we should not throw the blame on the poor girl.

Nze Okeke

White man you are the biggest problem in this village now. This issue is above you and your god. Ogbondu is a spirit of destruction when provoked. I am old enough to be your grand father. The only thing that can appease him now is the release of that girl. I have done the best I can to a friend. I am going home now.

[*As he moves he turns to Ebuka*]

Any person the gods want to kill they first make him mad.

[*With that statement he leaves the house*]

Johnny

[*Goes straight to where Chief Adaka lay and places his hand on his forehead and starts to pray with authority*]

Father in the name of Jesus Christ, I take authority over the life of this man. I stand against every plan of the enemy against Chief Adaka and his family. I command you now , spirit of Ogbondu or whatever you are called to pack your things and get out of this body in the name of Jesus.

SCENE 42

IN THE SPIRIT WORLD

The sprit of Ogbondu drags Chief's spirit to a desert place. There they tie him up with fitters of iron and chains. With the help of other demons he is being tormented. They are beating him with iron cord and chains. After a short period of time the prince raises his hand for them to stop the beating which they did.

Prince

I will use you and your family as an example to teach the whole village that Ogbondu never dies

[*He starts to hit him again*].

Chief
[*Weeping and pleading*]-

Please give me another chance. Please don't touch my family. Leave them alone. I promise to take appropriate action if you give me another chance.

[Using special effect Johnny's prayer is shown while this activity is going on with a great lightening followed by thunder and at the background of all these noises is a heavenly music THE ALLILUHA CHORUS. The sky at this moment is filled with angelic beings accompanying the Son of God. This time the music stops and a noise thundered Voice—THOU SHALL NOT WORSHIP ANY OTHER GOD BUT ME.

At the presence of the Son of man all other spirits including the prince of Ogbondu fell down and covered their faces. This time Chief is led into a weeding hall. Immediately he walks in he sees Ebuka his son at the entrance of the hall dressed in a wedding suit anger and confusion written all over his face.

Ebuka—

Daddy where have you been you are the one we are waiting for.

[Chief Adaka takes his son by the arm and leads him through the aisle gradually they moved in tune to the music to the waiting arm of Lynda

> *Music—Jesus—Blessed—Jesus*
> *. I love—That—Name*
> *I Love That Name*
> *Jesus—Blessed Savior*
> *There is no other name—I Know.*

[As the bride and bridegroom kiss each other the congregation goes into jubilation.

SCENE 43

Johnny

[*After the prayer*]

Ebuka bring the car to the front door

[*To Obidia*]

Collect materials like clothes and other things because you might be required to stay more days with him.

[*Ebenezer and Akilika are helping Johnny to sit him up. It was at this stage that his spirit is shown by special effect entering his body. This time he starts to breathe seriously, opens his eyes, starts to cough and sneeze at the same time.*]

Obidia

Oh my God he is awake

[*This time he manages to sit up properly on the bed*].

Johnny

[*Full of smiles*]

Chief are you all right? We are just making plans to send you to the hospital.

[*This time Ebuka comes in and is surprised to see him sitting on the bed*]

Chief

[*Managing to smile*]

There is no need for that now. I am okay. I believe we have come towards the end of this business. Where are my council of elders?

Ebuka
They have all gone home.

Chief

Yes! In fear of what Ogbondu might do. Including Nze Okeke and Aka Dike. White man I saw your Jesus during my journey to destruction. He gave me one particular instruction, which I must obey now

[*This time he stands up and starts to put on his clothes*]

. Ebuka where is the girl go and bring her to me.

[*There is surprises and confusion in the faces of those around*]

Johnny
What kind of instructions did he give you and why do you want Lynda now.

Chief
You don't need to fear. I mean no harm. I know she is some where in this compound. Call her for me1 She is part of the instruction.

[*Ebuka leaves them and goes straight to his room*]

SCENE 44

Ebuka is surprised to see his room open from a far distance. He goes in hurriedly but could not see Lynda. He goes under the bed but can not see her. He even searches the wardrobes but she is no where to be found. Ebuka becomes very alarmed. He rushes outside only to notice his half sister Nkechi withdrawing back in a hurry into her room opposite his.

Ebuka

[Shouting her name at the top of his voice]

. NkECHI! NKECHI!

. *[He rushes immediately into her room and pulls her out]*

. Where is the girl?

<u>Nkechi</u>

I don't know. Leave me alone.

Ebuka

[He lifts her up and starts to pound her.]

You must tell me where is she?

[At this stage Nkechi's mother comes out and holds Ebuka by the shirt.

<u>Second Wife</u>

If you must kill her you must kill both of us now. Leave her alone.

[*This time Ada Aku, Ebuka's sister comes out and sees what is going on she joins the fight. The noise attracts chief, Johnny, Ebenezer and the rest of chief's household. They all join hand to bring calm*

Chief Adaka
Ebuka I told you to call the girl and not to beat up your sister.

Ebuka
She is not there and she seems to know something about her whereabouts.

Chief
Nkechi where is the girl?

Nkechi
Nze Okeke and Aka Dike came with some young men and took her away.

Johnny.
Oh my God. Where did they take her?

Chief
It is okay. Who told them she is in this house?

[*They all keep silent*].

I say, how did they know she is hiding in the palace.

[*It is at this stage chief's second wife comes in.*]

Second Wife
Yes I brought them in because they told us that the only way to save you is to hand over the girl to the shrine.

Chief
And you are the proper person to hand over another person's daughter to the gods. Why didn't you tell them to take your own daughter if your love for me is that much. Thank you for saving my life.

[*Turning to Akilika*]

Call my driver. Let us hurry to the shrine.

[*They all started to leave in a hurry.*

SCENE 45

AT THE SHRINE
Lynda is bundled from the back of a pickup van. The van is covered all over. Five men lead her into a room. Inside the room she is handed over to three old women who look more like spirits than human.

First Woman
Please our queen sit down I hope they did not treat you bad.

<u>Second Woman</u>
Please my daughter don't cry. Nobody is going to harm you. We are here to ensure nothing bad happens to you.

Young men you can now go and leave her alone. Tell Obidia she will be fine.

[*The men who brought her leave the room*].

<u>Linda</u>

[*She looks at the old women and at the room and back to them*]

Please where am I and why am I here.

<u>Third Woman</u>

My child you have nothing to fear. You are going to stay here with us for safe keeping until the whole issue is settled.

<u>Lynda</u>

Who told them to bring me here?

<u>Third Woman</u>

Obidia of course. She wants us to protect you from the Elders. Tomorrow morning his son Ebuka will come and spend some time with you.

[In a low tone]

May be you will want to spend some time alone with him. Won't you?

[*They all laugh even Lynda is forced to smile. After this she seems to relax*]

<u>First Woman</u>

My little angel I know you must be feeling hungry.

[*She takes an already boiling kettle and adds some tea inside. She opens a cupboard and brings out four cups and gives one each to the women and one to Lynda. One after the other she pours tea in their cups but when she comes to Lynda's turn*

<u>Second Woman</u>

My daughter what is your name?

Lynda

Lynda—[*It is at this time of distraction that the old woman drops a small object into Lynda's cup.*

<u>Second Woman</u>

What a beautiful name to a beautiful face. No wonder even the gods must fight to win her.

[*They all laugh again even Lynda seems to be enjoying the jokes.*]

[*After an interval of 10seconds Lynda drops her cup and falls asleep*]

SCENE 46

Chief and his entourage stop at a few poles from the shrine and decide to walk. This time it is getting very dark. From where they stand they see some members of the church including Mary, Lynda's parents and some villagers in a scuffle. Two men are struggling with Lynda's father. They are trying to disarm him.

[This time chief and his group come in]

Chief—
Mazi Okwuonu it is okay everything will be fine now.

First Villager
Now I believe Ogbondu is a dead God. No person is ever forced into bridal moonlight ceremony.

Second Villager
How are we sure the girl is the choice of the gods. If so the gods should be allowed to take action.

Chief
Please every body should be quiet for the first time in my life I really want to see what is going on in that shrine.

[With Chief Adaka leading they all start to move towards the shrine]

SCENE 47

At the inner temple of the shrine Lynda is shown in bed dressed in white cloths the bed is surrounded with candles of different colors. The inner council members are dancing round the bed in response to the beating of the drum. At this stage a door at the left hand side to the bed opens and the chief priest comes out with a life cobra in his hand. The moment he enters the arena the music stops.

The Chief Priest
[He raises his voice and the serpent high and starts to make incantations]

.Greetings to you our great prince. For you are the custodian of the eastern gateway. The Eze Iru Agbarakata One. The thunder face. This is the bride of the covenant you made with our forefathers before the foundation of this earth was laid. Today we witness the unbroken bond between Ogbondu and his people. No man can break this bond.

[As he was about to put the head of the serpent between her legs the door of the temple bursts open.

The villagers and some members of the church led by Chief Adaka walk in. Ebuka is the first to attack the chief priest with a machete. He drops the snake and ran for his life. Lynda's father takes another machete and cuts off the snake's head. Johnny and Mary run to the cane bed and rescue Lynda. Akilika and the other chief's bodyguards prevent the chief priest from running away.

Nze Okeke
Chief what are you doing? We are here to save your life.

Chief Adaka

The God of the white man saved my life and that same God gave me some specific instructions, which I have come to carry out now. First this girl you see now

[pointing at Lynda in Mary's arm] is my daughter in law. I will announce the day of the wedding later.

Aka Dike

Adaka Ogwumagana are you crazy? Do you want to destroy your family?

Chief

I am not because I saw this God with my two eyes when I was going down the death road you in particular sent me.

Secondly—Today I am joining the villagers to announce the end of Ogbondu in Edeani. I am only giving every one of you 20 minutes to pack your things and leave this shrine.

Thirdly

[Turning to Johnny]

White man I Chief Adaka Ogwumagana the warrant chief of Edeani has authorized you to build your church in this place.

Finally I join the international committee on human right to ban the age long practice of caste system in Edeani. From today every person formerly regarded as untouchable or outcast is now a free born?

[The villagers and church members all start to jubilate and to sing.]

> Song—There is power—There is power
> There is power in the blood of Jesus.

[As they are all singing and moving out Chief gives a sign to Akilika who immediately calls the other bodyguards aside. Later they are seen pouring gasoline all over the shrine. Within 20minutes the whole shrine goes into flame.

WRITTEN BY BROTHER JONATHAN EZEMEKA

THE END

THIS SCRIPT IS DEDICATED TO ALL MISSIONARIES SERVING GOD IN DIFFERENT PART OF THE WORLD

Contact
Jonathan Ezemeka
Email : *i4jeo@yahoo.com*

THE ULTIMATE ASSIGNMENT

SCENE 1

At James Okafor, s house the wife Mrs. Uche Okafor is seen cleaning the whole room collecting both her husband's clothes and hers for washing. It is while she is doing this that a letter falls from one of her husband's clothes. She picks it up and read as follows—

[She can only read the following lines when she sees her husband coming—she falls down in front of him and starts to weep]

> *LETTER VOICE—My son I am daily coming nearer to my grave and I sincerely wish to see my grand child before I die. For ten years I have waited but without success. I am now asking you to come home and take another wife.*

Mrs.Uche—*[Dropping the letter before her husband and weeping at the same time]*

Oh James my dear if marrying another wife will solve your problem why not do it.

James Okafor—*[Taking her into his arm and sitting her on a couch]*

My dear the letter was written for me to take action but I have not. I have a place in mind to take you to—and I believe our visit to that place will yield fruits. Please don't be upset by my father's letter, everything will be all right.

Uche Okafor—*[Looking at her husband]*

I am ready to give my life in place of a child for you—Oh James what ever you want me to do I will do it.

James Okafor—*[He looks at her and remembered when he made marriage vows to her].*

FLASH BACK

[Uche and James were seen in there wedding clothes]

Pastor—*[Holds a bible in one hand and the couples in another]*

James Okafor wills thou have this woman to be thy wedded wife to live together after God's ordinance in the holy estate of matrimony? Will thou love her, comfort her, honor and keep her in sickness and in health forsaking all others keep thee only unto her, so long as you both shall live.

James Okafor—I will [*Looking at her in the eyes*]

SCENE 2

James and his wife are seen barefooted at the home of the native doctor who lives in the mountain. At the background of his shrine are stones of different sizes. Moving round the compound is a tortoise and a python. James and wife sit in fright.

Native Doctor [*Ringing a bell at intervals and hitting an empty tortoise shell*]

I am the bad water not fit for drinking. But when the thirst becomes unbearable I will then be good for drink. He who doesn't believe will do so when the problem defies human imagination.

Big church leaders and even small ones have all come to me when their prayers fails [*Laughs*] It is from them I learnt this saying—give to Caesar what is to Caesar and to God what is to God. [*Laughs again*]. [*This time he looks seriously at Uche*]

Woman you have a marine husband and no power on earth can make you have a baby.

[*She slumped into her husband's arm*]

SCENE 3

WHITE GARMENT PRAYER HOUSE

Prophetess Ada Ora is seen leading James and his wife to a small river behind the church for a special prayer and sacrifice. Uche is seen carrying a calabash while James follows quietly behind them. At the riverbank is a small hut of which only the prophetess can enter.

Before going into the hut the calabash is given to her, she opens it and brings a letter addressed to the queen of the ocean.

Prophetess—[*She gives the letter to James*]

You are the one who wrote the letter—read it to the queen.

James Okafor—[*Reading the letter*]

Greetings to you Oh queen of the heaven and of the ocean. Our great mother who lives in the ocean—we come in humility to request for a fruit of the womb.

[*He drops the letter into the calabash and gives the calabash to the prophetess*].

Prophetess Ada Ora—[*She uses the calabash to touch the couples head, abdomen, feet and their private parts before going into the small hut with the calabash. Inside the hut is the statue of the queen of the ocean, a screen of white cloth, an altar with candles of different colors and a cross with a man hanging on it. With the letter in her hand, she raises her voice and starts to make incantations.*—]

Greetings to you our mother Queen of the ocean, the great queen of the universe who lives beneath the sea. I come in humility and in total submission to your will. Please this family is in great need of a child. They need your help. [*Raises her voice*]

You've raised me as your daughter and you've promised to answer my request anytime I come to you. I have served you diligently all these years and have never failed you. Now is the time to fulfill your promise. I need an answer to this woman's problem.

Your church which I am the leader needs this miracle to boost our image in this society. Please what powers are blocking her womb.

[*With special effect the queen appears on the screen*]

The Queen—Ada my daughter you've stepped into a dangerous ground. That woman is married to one of our members here in the spirit world. Anyone married to our spirit does not make a family in the physical world. If she does it might cost her life.

Prophetess Ada Ora—I don't care what happens to her—all we need is a baby for them.

The Queen—[*Fades away gradually*]

She will have a baby.

SCENE 4

4 MONTHS LATER
Mrs. Uche Okafor

[*Looking very happy and pregnant*]

King James, do you know what happened today at the anti-natal clinic, where I went for a check up?

James—How would I know?

Mrs. Uche Okafor—They told us about family planning but I got up and told them that family planning is not for me.

[*They both laughed*].

SCENE 5

At the hospital labor room Uche Okafor is seen under labor while the husband is seen walking up and down the corridor waiting for news. The moment he sees the doctor coming he rushes to him for clues.

Doctor—[*Leads him to his office*]

Please sit down Mr. Okafor. I have two news for you, first your wife gave birth to a bouncing baby girl and the baby is in a very good condition.

Secondly—I am very sorry we could not save your wife's life. She died as a result of over bleeding.

Mr. James Okafor could not bear it, he weeps like a baby. The doctor and nurse just look at each other and start to console her.

SCENE 6

17 YEARS LATER
James Okafor is seen in his house singing a tune.

James Okafor All other gods they are the works of men

You are the only God, there is none like you.

[At this moment Chiamaka his daughter walks in].

Chiamaka—Daddy God bless you.

James Okafor—Ah Chiamaka, my daughter God bless you too. How was today's fellowship?

Chipmaker—*[Dropping her bible on the table]*

Daddy wonders shall never end. Today's fellowship was full of miracles, signs and wonders. Two boys among those that waylaid me last time gave their lives to Christ. After service they came to me and begged for forgiveness. Daddy can you believe that.

James Okafor—*[Looking at her and nodding his head at the same time]* Chi my daughter with God all things are possible. I really thank God for what he is doing in your life. I hope you've forgiven them.

Chiamaka—*[With a smile]*

Yes I did. The bible says we should forgive others so that our own sins will be forgiven also.

James Okafor—Now tell me what happened in the fellowship today?

Chiamaka—The man of God talked about Cosmic Conflict.

James Okafor—What does that mean?

Using special effect the man of God is seen speaking with great power in a fellowship setting, talking on the topic Cosmic Conflict.

Rev. Ede—Cosmic Conflict is a spiritual warfare going on in the spirit realm and manifesting itself in the physical. Decisions made in the spirit realm determines our day to day actions. Therefore things we can not see with our naked eyes other wise known as spirits—controls what we see known as the physical. The problems of Nigeria and every other nations of this world are as a result of the out come of this conflict. The only solution lie in what the bible says in—

> *Voice—2nd chr.7: 14 If my people, which are called by my name, shall humble themselves, and pray, and seek my face, and turn from their wicked ways; then will I hear from heaven, and will forgive their sins, and will heal their land.*

I predict in the name of Jesus that a spiritual revival that will engulf the whole world will start in Nigeria. Our country is fortunate to be at the center of a worldwide move of the Holy Spirit. Finally brethren, the unusual events around the globe at present is a clear indications of the end of time.

The time when the wheat and the tars will be separated. The time when the saints will be taken away to the great beyond.

James Okafor—[*Very surprised*]

What a wonderful topic. Thank God you were there. Oh how I wish your mother had the opportunity of knowing Christ before her death.

Chiamaka—*[A little anger written on her face]*

Daddy I have told you to stop calling on a mother I don't even know about. *[She gets up and starts to move towards the kitchen]*

I am going to prepare our meal.

[As she leaves the father continues to look at her in deep thought].

SCENE 7

FLASH BACK
James's mind went to the time of mourning for his wife. He was seen seated in a black mourning dress with shaved hair, sitting in a round table conference with his married sisters and their husbands.

Mr. Udechukwu
[*Husband to James elder sister*]

I am standing on behalf of other In-laws of yours to convey a decision we reached concerning your little daughter. Our people say that those who remain when a corpse has started to decay are the real Owners. Tears does not allow me to say much—our decisions are as follows

[1] Starting with my wife your elder sister—she will spend a month looking after your daughter

[2] After her your second sister mama Ada will follow and then Mama Udo. They will continue in this order till the child will be big enough to stay with you.

Turning to the others

I hope I have said it all.

They all nodded in agreement.

SCENE 8

Chiamaka has just entered with a plate of food only to notice the father struggling with pains in his chest. She drops the plate and runs to him.

Chiamaka—Daddy what is that? Has the chest pain come again?

James Okafor—Oh—my God—this particular pain is very devastating and it is choking me. Please help me to the chair.

This time he starts to foam and his eyes bulging Chiamaka starts to shout for neighbors who came in and helped to lie him on a bed. Within 30mins they organized an ambulance to take him to the hospital.

SCENE 9

IN THE SPIRIT WORLD

In what looks like a temple, beautifully designed sat more than 20 witches and wizards in different shapes and sizes.

Queen—*[Her eyes moving from place to place]* The prophecy—The prophecy

> *Voice—Joel 2: 28 And it shall come to pass afterwards that I will pour out my spirit upon all flesh and your sons and daughters shall prophesy—Your old men shall dream dreams, your young men shall see visions.*

I am now telling every one of you that this prophecy has come to place in our midst. We must act otherwise it will have a devastating effect on our operation on this earth. The signs we are receiving continue to show there is a great force contrary to our plan coming to rest in one of our human agent's home. The signs show that Chief Udofia's home is at the center of this havoc.

This time she starts to speak in strange tongues while with special effect Akwaeke Chief Udofia's wife is seen sleeping in her bed. With the same effect she is seen leaving her body as a cobra and at the same time appearing in the presence of the Queen and her members as Akwaeke. She is seen kneeling before them.

The Queen—Either you or your husband has arranged to bring confusion into your house. You are our only link to the outside world. From now on no visitor should spend a night in your home till further notice because we are still monitoring the situation.

If you make any mistake I will reduce your household to that of a street beggar.

SCENE 10

IN THE HOSPITAL BED
James is seen on the bed with IV passing into his arm. He looks really weak and breathes with effort; Chiamaka is seen sitting nearer to his bed her eyes red from crying.

James—Please help me to sit up.

[As Chiamaka tries to help him sit up, the door opens and Chief Udofia comes in]

Chiamaka—Oh—Uncle may God bless you. Daddy has been waiting for you. He is very sick.

Chief Udofia—*[looks surprised on seeing his condition]*

Oh my God—King James what is wrong with you. The language in your mail told me something terrible has happened. I came on a chattered flight *[This time shaking his head]*

I knew something bad is going on. King James I hope you will survive this?

James [*With great effort*]

Please sit down

[*Pointing to the only visitor's sit*]—

Chiamaka please go outside and wait.

[*When she left*]

Chief my daily prayer is that God should touch and reveal himself to you.

Chief Udofia I hope so but I know you did not take all these pains only to invite me for that and you did not send your daughter out for that also.

James—You are right—as you can see I may not survive this one. I sent her out because She has cried enough. Please chief Udofia I am making this request to you from my dead bed if anything happens to me I need your assistance to enable her complete her studies.

[*With an effort he brings out a small purse which he gives to him*]

This is all that is left of my pension's money.

FLASH BACK

Chief Udofia [*Chief's mind went back to the war front during Nigeria civil war when he got wounded and other soldiers left him and ran away only James took the risk and brought him* *out of danger. He came to his senses when James starts to shake violently like one struggling to gain air. He quickly opens the door]*

Chiamaka please call the nurse.

Within some few seconds nurses are seen attending to James who seems to be making his final battle with death. When the doctor comes in James looks very calm, after examination the doctor confirms him dead as a result of heart failure. Chiamaka falls on his bed and weeps bitterly while chief is seen consoling her and taking her out of the room.

SCENE 11

A maid lets Chiamaka into Chief Udofia.s living room. This time she is seen standing when Akwaeke Chief's wife comes in.

Akwaeke—[*Holding the young girl on her shoulder*]

Yes what can I do for you?

Chiamaka—[*Looking very surprised*]

Oh auntie it is me Chiamaka.

Akwaeke—And then what do you want here?

[*This time the chief walks in and on seeing Chiamaka he takes his wife aside into a room*].

Chief Udofia—[*Guides her to sit on the bed*]

Please my dear I really want you to understand the issue at stake. This is the daughter of a friend I cannot refuse to help. Before his death I promised to take care of his only daughter.

Akwaeke—I am sorry she cannot stay a night in this house.

Chief Udofia—[*Very surprised*] Why?

Akwaeke—I had a bad dream about this girl last night and I see great danger ahead if she stays a night in this house.

Chief Udofia—In short I owe my life today to the father of this girl. His father saved my life during the war. I promise she may not stay long, we may find her a job or admission into a school. Besides you are free to give her conditions for her stay. Let us go my dear.

[*Almost dragging her to the living room*].

Akwaeke—We have agreed to have you on the following conditions

[1] You must be of good behavior.
[2] On Sunday you must go to church with every member of the family.
[3] You must take the little ones to Sunday school every Sunday.
[4] Finally we shall not tolerate any other fellowship in this house.

[*After saying this she walks away*].

Chief Udofia—*[Shakes his head]* Don't worry my dear I know one day you both will come to understand each other. Just relax for she will show you your room. *[He leaves]*

Chiamaka—*[She just sat alone in deep thought]*

> *Voice—Fear not for I am with you be not dismayed for I am your God. I will strengthen you, I will help you, and I will uphold you with the right hand of my righteousness. I have made you an instrument of valor—You are my battle-axe. I will use you to pull down kingdoms. Don't panic for I am your God. I will never fail nor forsake you. Just be holy for I am holy.*

Akwaeke—*[She is seen standing at the door watching her with great interest]*

Come and see your room.

[Akwaeke's voice brings her to her senses. she gets up and follows her to a fairly furnished room. When Akwaeke leaves, she locks the door kneels down and starts to pray]

PLOT 12

IN THE SPIRIT WORLD
[The Queen is seen in the presence of her aids and she looks very angry].

Queen—I gave that idiot Akwaeke a simple instruction and she has failed. Now the presence of that girl in chief's house is going to distort our communication with the physical world.

[*She raises her hand and dark smoke starts to come out of her mouth. With special effect Akwaeke is seen leaving her body with the body of a cobra crawling out of her body to the floor. With the same effect she appears as Akwaeke in the spirit world kneeling before the queen*]

You must do every thing within your power to frustrate her out of your home before we loose our contact with you. I say you must not allow her in that house. Now go

Akwaeke—[*Looks frightened*]

Please how will I do that so as not to raise my husband's suspicious because keeping her means life and death promise he made to the father before his death. Please I need your advice.

Queen—[*Turning to her aids*]

You hear her! That she needs advice. Our principal agent to the physical realm needs advice to deal with a small girl. What will you tell other agents under you?

First Spirit—You must direct the spirit of lust and fornication to her.

Second Spirit—You send her spirit of frustration to frustrate her spiritually.

Third spirit—You must find a way to lure her into our group.

Akwaeke——Please the sex option should be ruled out because from what I have observed in her. She seems to be serious with her faith in God.

Queen—Then you must find some one amongst our members to help shift her faith from the real truth. If every thing fails you must use force. This is your last chance. Now go

[*She raises her hand and blows smoke*]

SCENE 13

AT CHIEF UDOFIA'S HOUSE
Chiamaka [*Is seen washing plates in the kitchen and singing at the same time*]

> He is the Lord. He is the Lord—Amen
> He has risen from the dead.
> He is the Lord
> Every knee shall bow—Every tongue confess that Jesus
> Christ is the Lord.

[*She stops singing when she notices someone standing at the door singing with her*].

Chika—[*Comes in and stands in front of her smiling*]

Chiamaka God bless you.

Chiamaka—[*Very surprised*]

And bless you too.

Chika—As a fellow believer Madam wants me to always keep you company at least we can always share things in common.

Chiamaka—[*Seems to compose herself with a smile*]

Oh that's very good of her. You sing very well. And I love your voice.

Chika—Thanks for appreciating my voice, with time I will help you develop yours. I am really sorry Madam told me you lost both your father and mother.

Chiamaka—That's okay God has given me the strength to overcome the losses.

Chika—I hope to see more of you. I just came to say hi. I am going for choir practice.

[*She left*]

Chiamaka—[*After Chika has left she feels cold and fear all over her body*]

Oh my God what is causing these fears in me? Oh God my Lord you are the rock on which I stand. This house is full of fears and uncertainty.

> *Voice thought*—*Beware of false prophets who go about in sheep's clothing but inwardly they are wolves.*

Thinking loud—No—No—I can't believe that.

Chika doesn't look false to me—If she is—who then is saved

[She looks around the kitchen in fear. This time Akweke stands at the door in her nightgown. Chiamaka looks at her face and there is a flash. She sees in her face just in a moment of time a cobra ready to strike. This picture to her disappears and appears at will.

Chiamaka looks shocked but continues to move backwards gradually. She opens her mouth to shout but could not say a word. Akwaeke continues to move towards her. It is only when Chiamaka mistakenly hits the kitchen table full of plates and they fall with great noise that she leaves slamming the door. Chiamaka sits on the kitchen floor weeping.

SCENE 14

Chiamaka is seen surrounded by the chief's children Kene and Tochi in the living room.

Chiamaka—Do you know that God loves children? I want every one of you to believe that God loves you as a person.

Kene—Chi why is it that mummy does not like to pray?

Chiamaka—It is our duty to pray for our parent's daily.

Tochi—We heard you crying in the kitchen yesterday night did mummy beat you?

At this stage Akwaeke comes in with pastor Okere—a man at his late 50s.

Akwaeke—Chiamaka Please forgive me for what happened yesterday night. I don't even know what is wrong with me. The pastor has just finished praying for me and he wants us to live in peace. I hope you'll forgive me.

[*Chiamaka looks at her and then at the pastor before nodding her head*].

Pastor Okere—[*Smiling and still looking at her*]—Forgive and you will be forgiven. I wanted to spend a few moment with you to at least strengthen you in faith. Hope you wouldn't mind?

Chiamaka—[*Smiling also*]

Its okay with me.

Pastor—[*Looking at her straight in the eyes*].

Chiamaka I am very impressed with what I hear about your faith in God

Akwaeke—[*Interrupts*] Chi after your discussions with him I want you to deposit this 10000 naira for me at the bank near the T—junction supper market.

[*This time she hands her some money and her bank note.* Take a taxi and stop at the T-junction supper market

[*After this she left them*].

Pastor—Yes my dear—you need to be guided in faith and to be given a sense of direction so that you will not be in conflict with others.

In the first place every person has a right to God almighty even Muslims, Buddhists, Catholics, Anglicans, Hindus, and even atheist just to name a few. We are the creatures of this wonderful God.—[*He pauses and looks at her*]—Yes you want to say something.

Chiamaka—[*Looks surprised*] Sir but the bible says that unless one accepts Jesus Christ as Lord and personal savior he cannot see the Kingdom of God.

Pastor—Yes my dear you are right

[*Still smiling at her*]

In John's gospel

> Voice—*John 1:1,14. In the beginning was the word and the word was with God and the word was God. And the word was made flesh and dwelt among us and we beheld his glory, the glory as of the only begotten of the father full of grace and of truth.*

Therefore if Christ is the word what is needed is your obedience to this word that means accepting Christ

Secondly my dear every thing on this earth is subject to negative and positive forces depending from which point of view you are looking at it. Name it—the motorcars, electricity, religion, money and so on. Judge not so that you will not be judged.

[He stops and looks at her]

Any question?

Chiamaka—Yes I have a comment. Sir in the first place the bible says in

> *Voice—1 john 4:1—3*
> *Beloved, believe not every spirit, but try the spirits whether they are of God; because many false prophets are gone out into the world. Hereby know you the spirit of God; every spirit that confesseth that Jesus Christ is come in the flesh is of God. And every spirit that confesseth not that Jesus Christ is come in the flesh is not of God: and this is that spirit of antichrist, wherefore yea have heard that it should come; and even now already is it in the world.*

[She closes the bible and looks at him]

Sir how do you think any one can effectively obey this word without acknowledging Christ human nature first. I strongly believe Satan does not want us to accept this truth that God could fall so low as to come in human flesh.

Secondly sir the bible says in—

> *Voice Genesis 2:16—But of the tree of the knowledge of good and evil Thou shall not eat of it: for in the day that thou eatest thereof thou shall surely die.*

From what the bible says the release of energy through the interplay of negative and positive is not the truth but death to mankind. The missing link is—that tree of life which can make one live for ever. Obedience starts with beliefs. I'll read another passage for you.

> *Voice John 6:47 Verily, Verily, I say unto you, He that believeth on me hath everlasting life.*

Sir you will agree with me the issue rests on believing first and then doing and not doing without believing. All religion teach and do same but as long as they do not accept the divinity of Jesus Christ they are not of God. Finally sir Christianity is not a religion but a personal relationship with a living God.

[*At this stage the pastor gets up, scratches his head and left while Chiamaka gets up and goes to the children*].

SCENE 15

Chiamaka opens the front gate and waves the first taxi to a stop. She goes in and locks the door.

Chiamaka—[*She is surprised to see two people in the car—a man in front and a girl at the back*].

I am stopping at the T—junction supermarket.

Driver—They are stopping at the next junction.

[*He moves on but after some time he stops the car opens the car boot and brings out a tool spanner. He goes to the bonnet and does some repairs before returning the tool to the boot. He gets in starts the car and moves on. After a time he stops again and off the engine. Through out this period Chiamaka looks confused but calm.*

The Driver—

[*He turns his attention towards the girl*]

What is in that box you are carrying?

Chiamaka—[*Very surprised*]

How does what she is carrying concern you?

The Driver—Suppose that box contains drug or something dangerous, do you know we are all going to be involved. I know from where I picked her and till now she does not even know where she is going. Please you people should help me ask this girl where she is going and what is in that big and expensive box that she is carrying. I don't want to stop my business to answer any police questions.

The Strange Man—Hi girl what is in that box and where the hell are you going to stop?

Chiamaka—[*Very impatient*] Why not tell the driver at least where you are going. Please driver if you don't want to go I will drop out here and find another taxi.

The Strange Man—Tell us what is in that box? Do you want to put all of us in trouble?

The Young Girl—The box belongs to my boss whom I was living with as a maid. I heard from the news this morning that he died in a plane crash with his wife. I am taking the box home for safekeeping.

The Driver—What is the content of that box?

The Young Girl—I believe money.

The Strange Man—How much do you think it contains?

The Girl—They wrote with a piece of paper attached to it 3million.

[*The two men shout! Chiamaka turns in surprise and looks at her*]

The Strange Man—What the hells are you going to do with that amount of money?

The Young Girl _—There is a charm attached to the box. I want to take it home and find a native doctor who will neutralize its effect.

The Driver—[*Turning to the passengers*] Now she is talking—equal participation means equal taxation. I can help find a very powerful native doctor that will neutralize what ever charm no matter how strong it might be but first thing first—what is our own share. I promise no one will report to the police.

The Strange Man—[*Turning to Chiamaka*]

This is a very big opportunity for every one of us in this taxi to become rich. At least we can split it 50/50. She gets 50% while three of us split the rest.

Chiamaka—Stop me here for I am not interested [*turning to the girl*] A small girl like you stole the money that belongs to your dead boss. I just pray that God forgives you.

[*She opens the door and as she is about to go out the young girl takes Chiamaka's purse, pushes her out of the car and locks the door while the driver drives off. Chiamaka shouts and runs towards the car but no way they have gone with the money. She sits down helplessly on the road crying. A handful of people gather round to console her.*]

PLOT 16

CHIEF'S HOUSE
Chiamaka is seen weeping while Akwaeke is seen rebuking her.

Akwaeke—I can't understand what you are saying. You mean my 10000naira have gone like that? Shit I told chief your presence here is going to bring disaster.

[*Chiamaka wants to explain but Akwaeke does not give her any chance to say something. This time chief is seen coming out with traveling bags and at the same time talking to some one on his cell phone. When he notices the anger on his wife's face, he drops his bag.*]

Chief Udofia—What is the matter again?

[*Before Chiamaka can say anything, Akwaeke has already started to speak.*]

Akwaeke—I can't understand this girl you brought here. The 10000naira I gave her to just deposit into my account is gone. Em—that she entered a taxi and saw two people a man and a girl. Em—the girl is carrying 3million—in short she is just telling me a cock and bull story.

Chief Udofia—[*Interrupts*] Oh my God! Chiamaka I am sorry you were not fully briefed. This city is full of con men popularly known as 419, sorry my dear for the embarrassment they've caused you

[*He turned to his wife*]

Please my dear forgive her, remember she is just new in this town. I will replace the money for you when I come. Okay? I am rushing to catch a flight.

[*He kisses her and leaves*]

FLASH BACK

Akwaeke—[*kneeling down before the queen*]

Queen—If you fail—your family will beg bread in this city.

[*She looks at Chiamaka with great bitterness and walks out*].

SCENE 17

AT CHIEF'S HOUSE

Chiamaka is seen sleeping on her bed. With special effect she is at the ocean shore with Chika walking hand in hand smiling and laughing. From a distance they see Akwaeke coming towards them.

Chiamaka—Look at madam where is she coming from?

Chika—She told me she wants to make peace with you.

[This time Akwaeke comes to them, holds Chiamaka's hand and smiles at them].

Akwaeke—*[Still smiling]* Chi I am sorry for what happened yesterday I lost my temper. Please I hope you will forgive me?

[This time again Chiamaka looks and behold from the same direction comes one like a mermaid walking towards them. She wears a very long hair almost touching the sea sand she held a golden staff with flat top and three self-standing legs.

Chiamaka is terribly shaken when she sees this figure coming towards them.

Akwaeke—*[Still smiling]* you need not to fear my dear she means no harm.

[When the queen came Akweke and Chika bow down before her but she ignores them and goes straight to place her golden staff in front of them. She then takes Akwaek's hand, Chika's

and Chiamaka's and brings out a golden cord and starts to tie them together. Chiamaka is the only one who looks frightened while Akwaeke and Chika seems to be enjoying the whole thing. She keeps their hands on the flat top of the staff. She then brings out something like a chocolate, which she drops one into Akwaeke's mouth, Chika's mouth. But when she came to Chiamka's turn she shakes her head and shouts].

Chiamaka—Blood of Jesus!

[At the mention of that name heaven seems to let loose. There is an explosive noise. Smoke files the whole area. The queen herself is no where to be found. Chika and Akwaeke fall on the floor.

[When the smoke clears Akwaeke and Chika are seen dusting their bodies.

Akwaeke—*[Is very furious, angry and with great effort she gets up and faces Chiamaka]*

Who told you to mention that name in her presence?—You idiot she could have secured your position in our home.

[At this stage, Chiamaka looks in her face and beheld a cobra ready to strike. She wakes up from her sleep with a great noise. This time she gets up from her bed and runs out of the room. Already the noise has woken Akwaeke who sleeps in the next room and who already came out to see what is going on. Outside her room Chiamaka comes face to face with Akwaeke coming out from her bedroom. She shouts again and runs out of the building.

SCENE 18

CHIEF UDOFIA'S HOUSE
Akwaeke and Chika are seen seated on the dining table.

Chief Udofia—[*Comes later and sits at the head of the table*]

My dear I can't really understand what you are telling me. No person touched Chiamaka that you heard a noise and you came to see what was wrong then she saw you and ran out of the room. Whom do you think will believe that? The little I know about that girl is that she does not show any sign of insanity.

Chika—Chief to be frank you need to do more investigation about that girl. She might be a silent killer. The first day I met her she really doesn't show any sign of anger but to run away without cause is something else.

Akwaeke—My dear I predicted this girl's problem before but you as usual refused to listen to me. Now I think it is really getting out of hand. This issue has gone beyond human imagination—I know a very good spiritual church that might offer solutions to this evil that is creeping into our family.

Chief Udofia—I have no objections my concern is what people will say. The rumor now will be that Chief Udofia has used her to make money. I just want her back.

[At this stage Tochi and Kene came in.

Tochi—Mummy where is auntie Chiamaka we did not pray this morning.

Kene—I want auntie Chi to take me to school.

Akwaeke—[*Taking them into the room*] Auntie Chi is coming. I will take you my self—I sent her some where.

SCENE 19

AT A WHITE GARMENT CHURCH

The church band is playing life. People are in white garment dancing to the music. The MC a young lady that looks like a sea goddess is seen with a microphone and twisting her hip in a very provocative manner to the tone of the music.

Prophetess—[*Pointing to Chief Udofia and his entourage as they enter the church hall*

Mr. Man stop

[*They obeyed*]

Remove your shoes for the place you are about to enter is a holy place.

[*They obey as directed but this time another girl who seems as though possessed runs from the other end of the church and stops in front of them.*

Possessed Girl—[*Pointing at Chief Udofia while at the same time speaking in strange tongues*].

Prophetess—*[Seems to be interpreting what the possessed girl is saying]*

[1] That Chief Udofia's family has inherited a calamity meant for another family.
[2] The girl is going to be the cause of your downfall if you are not careful.
[3] She ran away because some evil forces possess her.
[4] She needs a very serious deliverance and cleansing.

When they finish the strange talk and its interpretations their main Leader comes and takes over the microphone from the prophetess. He wears a red garment; a special music ushers him in.

Chief Aladura—Chief Udofia you and your family must prepare for a sin offering tomorrow

[1] Sin as you all know is a stumbling block between God and man.
[2] Many pray for God's forgiveness without going through the proper channel therefore their prayers cannot be answered.
[3] Do not allow people deceive you—just calling the name of Jesus alone will not remove your sins. Then hardened criminals, highway bandits, murderers, prostitutes and the like need not to worry but just call the name of Jesus and then continue their business. God is not an author of confusion he did not establish the sin offering in Leviticus for nothing.

[*This time the music is special with trumpets. He is seen dancing to the tune and is joined by other church members.*

SCENE 20

IN TONY MARTIN'S HOUSE
They are newly married Christian couple in their well furnished home. The wife is seen setting the table for breakfast while the husband who has just entered from the room stands aside and watches.

Mrs. Martins—[*She stops and looks at him*]

Why look at me as if am the launch some thing bothering you?

Tony—[*Just takes her gently to a double sitter chair*]—Today is Monday isn't it?

Mrs. Martins—[*Very surprised but still looking at him*] Yes

Tony—I have a feeling God wants me to do something that is strange to me on Wednesday.

Mrs. Martins—How do you know it is on Wednesday?

Tony—Because I was coming back from office in the midnight and you know that every last Wednesday of the month is our monthly return and we usually close at midnight.

Mrs. Martins—And what do you think he wants you to do?

FLASH BACK

With special effects, Tony is seen driving at midnight and on approaching this big compound he saw from a distance a girl running out of this building. Chiamaka is seen running down the road in her nightgown. As Tony approaches she waves at him desperately. Tony wants to stop but later changes his mind and continues to move but later again stops as she runs to his car.

Mrs. Martins—It is the devil. Don't mind him he wants you to bring in a younger and more beautiful girl in the house. The next thing you will tell me is that God wants you to marry her. *[Still looking at her husband]* and Tony when have you started to use the name of God to satisfy your lust?

Tony—My dear we still have some days before Wednesday to pray for God's guidance. Let us pray. *[They held hands in prayer]*.

SCENE 21

PRAYER HOUSE
The Leader, Prophetess, and two other men in black were seen welcoming Chief and his wife for the sin offering

Chief Aladura—*[Speaking in strange tongue]* now—Chief present your materials for sin offering

Chief Udofia—I now present the following items as requested—the white ram without blemish, #25,000.

Chief Aladura—[*He takes the materials to the alter*]

He offers prayers in strange tongues before killing the ram with the help of the two men in black. The blood of the ram is sprinkled on the altar. He dips his hand into the blood and makes cross sign on the face of Chief and his wife.

The belly of the ram is opened and the money for the sin offering is dumped in inside and sealed.

Now let us go to the river for the proper sacrifice and cleansing.

SCENE 22

IN TONY MARTINS HOUSE
Tony is seen looking up himself in the mirror, trying to straighten his tie when his wife comes and holds him. Tony stops what he was doing turns around and they look at each other face to face.

Mrs. Martins—[*Tears trickling down her cheek*]. Tony I am sorry the way I spoke to you last time. The spirit of God warned me seriously to stop hindering the work of the Holy Spirit. I am ready to go with you to pick her up—who ever she might be.

Tony—[*They hold each other for a very long time*]

The battle is not physical but a spiritual warfare. Don't worry about that sometimes jealousy in the part of a woman is a sign of love. Now I will be rushing to the office,—just keep on praying—if it is the will of God I will surely come back with her.

SCENE 23

AT THE RIVER BANK
Aladura, Prophetess, the two men in black including Chief and his wife are seen at the riverbank. The ram and its content are placed near the riverbank.

Chief Alladura—[*Ringing a very big bell and speaks in strange tongue at intervals. He makes sign to chief who comes and kneels before him]. He then takes the ram and rotates it three times over his head. He does the same to the wife].*—

- Now chief you can now throw the ram into the river.
- [*Chief obeys*]
- Now let us go back to the church.

SCENE 24

STILL AT THE CHURCH
Chief Alladura is seen addressing Udofia and the wife.

Chief Alladura—You people have now thrown your sins into the river. Your whole family should fast and meditate on psalm 35. When you find the girl bring her for deliverance

[He raises his hand over them]

May the blessings of God guide and protect you all.

Church Members—Amen

Alladura—You can now go in peace.

[*Chief and wife leave*]

From a small door near the altar three members of the church bring the ram into the presence of the Alladura. The men open the ram and pours out the contents on the floor. The group goes into serious jubilation and dancing.

SCENE 25

IN THE SPIRIT WORLD
The Queen addresses some special agents on the end time events.

The Queen—We are now coming to the final battle, a time when it shall be very difficult for any person to buy or sell without been registered in our kingdom. Any one who is not for us is against us.

[*She raises her hand and blows smoke out of her mouth. Akwaeke appears in their palace trembling before her*].

Now you must go and rescue the girl from the hand of another agent of confusion in the town. Their case is kidnapping make no mistake about it.

[*She blows the smoke again and Akwaeke's spirit disappears she now turns to her members and starts to laugh*]

Their saying goes like this that every thing work for good for them that believes. That girl's case has brought them together.

[*She makes a sign of shooting*]

I will shoot them all with just one bullet.

[*This time she becomes very serious*] The bible says in—

> Voice—*Rev. 3:11—Behold I come quickly; Hold that fast which thou hast that no man take thy crown.*
[*She now looks at the members*]

Do you all know what that crown is?

The Agents—[*They all shake their heads*]

The Queen—The crown the bible is talking about is the kingdom that was initially given to our master Lucifer and now it has been assigned to these so called born again fools.

[*This time she speaks with anger*]—

To stop them is a task that must be done. I repeat our function is to stop them at all cost. I am charging every one of you to double up your efforts. We must destabilize them. Everything is under our control and they are at your deposals sex, money and power. As many as believe in our mission give them money, power and fun. Use as much as you can. Anywhere this seed is planted uproot it. I repeat we must stop them.

SCENE 26

TONY MARTINS HOUSE
In the morning Chiamaka is seen in the arm of Tony Martin's wife but still weeping. Tony sits opposite them.

Tony—It is okay—my dear stop crying. I thank God for making it possible for you to be here with us. The Holy Spirit just directed my wife and I to bring you here. We will want to here your story.

Mrs. Martins—*[Helping her to wipe her tears]*

My dear you are free with us. From now on your problem is our problem we must share every thing in common.

Chiamaka—[*Still wiping tears from her face*]

I am Chiamaka Okafor my mother died while giving birth to me. I was left with my sick father who died a year ego. Before he died he arranged my stay with Chief Udofia his wartime friend. It was while in this house I discovered that the wife is a marine spirit agent who manifest herself as a cobra at will. I ran away this night because she wants to initiate me into their cult.

[This time Tony and his wife are really shocked. It is also at this stage that their bell rings. Tony goes and opens the door for the pastor of their church. They all stand up and welcome him.

Tony—Pastor you are welcome. You came at a very right time. How is your family?

Pastor—They are fine. How about yours?

[*This time taking a seat*]

Mrs. Martins—Daddy what do I offer you—coke? Juice? Or just fruits?

Pastor—Coke is okay for me. Em—I am led by the spirit to give you words of encouragement. I don't know what you are facing now.

[*Seems to notice Chiamaka for the first time*] You have a visitor?

Mrs. Martins—Yes she is our visitor.

Tony—She was living with the popular Chief Udo Udofia but ran away when she found out the wife is a practicing witch. Even at this moment her life and ours seems to hang in a balance.

Pastor—[*Nodding his head while still looking at her*]

As Christians we should always bear in mind that many circumstances that looks odd in our lives are aimed at fulfilling. God's purpose. I was led by the spirit to share this passage with you.

> *Voice—Ephesians 6:11—12 Put on the whole armor of God, that ye may be able to stand against the wiles of the devil. For we wrestle not against flesh and blood, but against principalities, against powers, against the rulers*

of the darkness of this world, against spiritual wickedness in high places.

We are all facing a cosmic battle. My spirit tells me something big may come your way but what ever it is the passage wants you to know it is not a physical battle.

Let us pray

[*They all kneel down to pray*]

SCENE 27

TONY'S HOUSE

Tony is seen in his room dressing himself up for work while the wife and Chiamaka are seen preparing the table for breakfast suddenly their is an usual knocking at the door. Tony's wife and Chiamaka are very shocked and surprised. They stop all they are doing. This time Tony comes out from his room with his tie not properly done. At this stage the door bursts open and two policemen come in brandishing their gun at Tony. Two other policemen come into the house through the back door.

First Policeman—[*Pointing his gun at Tony*]

Hands up or I shoot you. I am arresting you on the order of the federal republic of Nigeria for kidnapping. Be quiet and say nothing for any thing you say will be used against you in the court of law.

Tony—[*Raised his hands*]

What have I done to deserve this treatment

Second Policeman—[*Putting the handcuff on him*]

You've heard what he said, "anything you say would be used against you in the court."

Tony and wife are taken into a waiting police van before Chiamaka can say a word she is taken to a car where she finds herself in the waiting hand of Chief and his wife.

Chief Udofia—[*To the driver*]

Take us home immediately.

SCENE 28A

AT THE POLICE STATION
The police van stops in front of the station. Tony and wife are violently pushed down and are still in handcuffs. They are later loosened and given papers to write their statement. They submit all their possessions; Tony is taken to the male section while a policewoman takes the wife to the female section.

SCENE 28B

AT THE MALE SECTION
Tony is pushed into a dark cell room full of inmates. One of them gets up in the darkness and comes towards him and pushes him roughly. At one corner of the cell sits the chief Kodo of the cell

Papa Uwa—[*Dragging him to meet Kodo*]

You must give honor to whom it is dew.

Kodo—[*Raising his voice very high*]

I need a chair this hard floor is paining me.

[*Two other inmates brings Tony to his presence and makes him to squat for the [Kodo to sit on him]*

Director of public persecution [DPP]

DPP—[*One inmate stands up]*

Yes sir

Kodo—What is this man's offence?

DPP—He is charged for kidnaping.

Kodo—[*He gets up from Tony]*

My friend stand up I should know every man capable of committing that kind of crime in this city.

[*He looks at him for sometime]*

Are you a kidnaper?

Tony—I did not kidnap any person.

[*This time other inmates pounce on him and want to rough handle him]*

Kodo—Leave him alone. My friend you can go now and sit down.

[*Tony goes to a corner and sits down*]

SCENE 29

IN PASTOR'S HOUSE
The pastor is seen writing on a table when his wife comes in and sits near to him.

Pastor's Wife—My dear do you know that Tony and his wife are under arrest for kidnapping.

Pastor—What do you mean?

Pastor's Wife—Some one who just came from the police station told me this morning.

[*At this stage Bro. Johnson and Sister Mary come in*].

Sister Mary—[*Giving him a newspaper*]

Do we have to believe this report—that Tony and his wife kidnapped a girl living with a millionaire—Chief Udofia.

Pastor—Please sit down I want to explain something to you all. I was in Tony's house two days ago. A night before that the spirit placed a burden on me to visit them and encourage them with this passage of the scripture

[*With special effect this passage was played on*

Voice—Ephesians 6:11—12] I was not able to understand the meaning of this until I went and saw this girl myself.

All—So it is true?

Pastor—No—Tony did not kidnap the girl. The girl is a strong believer. She ran away from Chief Udofia's house when she found out that chief's wife wants to initiate her into marine spirit cult. The problem is a spiritual problem; we should go into serious prayer for God's intervention. Meanwhile Sister Mary and Bro. Johnson should join me to visit chief's house to see what we can do. Let us pray.

SCENE 30

IN CHIEF UDOFIA'S HOUSE
Chiamaka is seen crying while Chief, Akwaeke and Chika are watching her.

Chief—[*Looking at Chiamaka*]

Do you know that Tony and his wife are responsible for all the missing people in this city.

Chiamaka—No—it is a lie I don't believe it.

Chief—Well that is what the police say about them.

Chiamaka—I know it is not true because I was safe in their house.

Chief Udofia—Do you mean you are not safe in this house. That reminds me why did you run away from my house in the first place.

[At this question Akwaeke becomes irritated and stands up]

Chiamaka—I saw *[She looks at Akwaeke and stops]*

Chief Udofia—Yes—say it out—why did you run away from my house?

Akwaeke—*[She sees the danger in this question and continues to look at Chiamaka.*

Chiamaka—[Looks at her and sees the same vision of a cobra ready to strike. This time she picks up courage]

I rebuke you in the name of Jesus I release the Holy Ghost fire on you.

Akwaeke falls down and starts to gyrate like a serpent. Chika runs out of the room. While Chief moves back in fear.

SCENE 31

IN CHIKA'S ROOM
She is packing some clothes into a box.

Chika—*[Very confused]*

If Akwaeke is discovered my life as a Christian is ruined in this city. I am leaving this city, I am fed up with this kind of life.

[*At this stage there is knocking at her door, she stops her parking in surprise*]

Who on earth is that?

[*This time the door opens and this gorgeously dressed lady walks in*].

Lady Ann—Where the hells do you think you are going Chika?

Chika—[*Confused and frightened*]

Do I know you? Who are you please? What do you want from me?

Lady Ann—[*She looks directly at Chika and with special effect Chika is able to see her clearly as she was during their encounter at the river bank. Chika falls down and faints. The lady sits down and waits. After a short time Chika recovers from her shock and bows before her three times*].

My daughter leaving this city will not solve your problem don't you know you are like a slave to me. I am the one who determines where you go. Well you have nothing to fear. I have come to straighten things myself. You must prepare your self to act as my special agent to the outside world. I will introduce you to the Ultimate Club. Be calm everything will be all right.

[*She opens her bag and brings a special invitation which she gives to her*]

With this invitation you are now a member of the elite club in this nation. Welcome to the Ultimate Club.

Chika—What will be the faith of Akwaeke?

Lady Ann—Just wait and see. She has failed us and she must pay for it.

[*She goes to the door and melts away*]

SCENE 32

CHIEF UDOFIA'S SITTING ROOM

Chiamaka is seen still shouting Holy Ghost fire and the blood of Jesus while Akwaeke is on the floor gyrating like a serpent. Chief is asking Chiamaka to move backwards. At this stage the doorbell rings Chief leaves her and goes to open the door for the pastor and his group. When the pastor comes in and sees what is going on he starts to speak in tongues joined by Sister Mary and Brother Johnson.

Akwaeke—[*With a male voice*]

I am not leaving this body.

Pastor—Who are you?

Akwaeke—[*With the same male voice*]

> *My name is Hatred and I hate God! I hate the son! I hate this woman! I hate the husband! Even you I hate you all! All human race I hate you all! Another male's voice, My*

name is anger! I am angry with God, his son, at the husband and every human race. Other voices—[Both male and female]—I am fornication, Adultery. I am greed; my name is suicide [and so many other].

Pastor—[*In a very quiet voice*]

Whether you like it or not you must leave this body. This body was purchased with the precious blood of Jesus Christ. The bible also says that our body is the temple of God. Therefore you have no right to be here. God revealed himself in Jesus Christ in order to destroy every work of your master the devil.

Akwaeke—[*Still in a male voice*]

voices—we are not leaving this body! If you like quote whatever thing you like. This body is our dwelling place. Nothing will move us from this body.

Pastor—[*In a very calm voice*]

At Calvary Jesus Christ was humiliated, bruised, nailed hand and feet blood was rushing all over him

[At this gruesome description the demons start to manifest through Akwaeke]

Akwaeke—[*Still using male voice*]

VoiceS—No ! No ! Don't mention that! We saw it all! None of us will want to remember what happened that day.

Pastor—[*Raises his hand and now speaking with authority*]

I command you in the mighty name of Jesus Christ to leave this body and go into the pit and never you enter any other human body again.

[*There's a great noise from Akwaeke and a cobra crawls from her body out of the house. Chief and others draw back in fear.*

SCENE 33

AT THE ULTIMATE PLAZA HOTEL

The banner displayed all over the place reads—ANNUAL GENERAL MEETING OF THE ULTIMATE CLUB.

Two stoned-faced men are seen at the gate accrediting members into the hall.

Inside this hall sits men and women that matter in the society. Lady Ann is seen addressing them.

Lady Ann—This meeting is for all our members who are in a position of authority in this country. The purpose of this meeting is for you to start from now taking decisions within your departments that will make it impossible for the present leadership to manage the nation. When this is done effectively the leadership of the country will be taken over by our members in the Ultimate Club. Mr. Bernard—you are the minister of education. **Mr. Bernard**

[*He stands up*]

Yes I am.

Lady Ann—Next week there is going to be a great student unrest. If that happens all you need to do is to close all the schools. Our agents in campus have arranged everything.

[*Bernard nods his head*]

Chief of custom and immigration services

[*A man stands up*]—

Now listen to me very carefully all containers entering into this country with questionable products must be seized especially those belonging to none members.

Chief Tax Officer and police chief organize a raid on those owing huge amount of money to the government. Their properties should be sold to recover the amount they owe.

[*Looking towards the direction of Chika who sits by her side*]

From today Akwaeke is an enemy of this club any one dealing with her on our behalf is doing so on his or her own risk. This girl Chika

[*pointing at her*] is now my personal assistant.

[*This time she starts to leave the hall and all the members stand up for her. As she moves she beckons to a man*]

Chief of police

[*who came and bowed before her*] see me now for a very special assignment.

SCENE 34

POLICE CHIEF'S OFFICE

The police chief is sipping a steaming tea. He presses the intercom and a police officer brings in Kodo, salutes him and leaves. Kodo still under handcuffs stands and watches him sipping his tea in silent

Police Chief—You may sit down. [*Kodo sits down*]

What offences were you charged of?

Kodo—Armed robbery sir.

Police Chief—And if you are convicted this crime caries the death penalty.

[*Still looking at him from his steaming cup of tea*].

I have a job for you and if you do it well I will submit your case file to the armed robbery tribunal with lack of evidence.

Kodo—What kind of job sir?

SCENE 35

IN UDOFIA'S HOUSE

Akwaeke has just recovered sits down weeping like a baby while Chiamaka consoles her.

Chief Udofia—[*Talking to the Pastor*]

What do you think is wrong with her? You mean for the past years I have lived with a serpent as a wife?

[*He is almost in a state of panic*].

Oh my God—why me?

[*He sits down*]

Pastor—[*Ignoring chief*]

Madam you've seen what a great thing God has done in your life. Are you now ready to accept Christ into your life to replace that evil spirit that has just left? Will you now invite him to take control of your life or do you still want your life to be controlled by agents of devil and Satan himself.

Chief Udofia—[*Full of anger*]

Upon all the love I gave you! You hid this from me.

Akwaeke—[*Wiping tears with her hand*]

Right from child hood I have been a marine spirit agent. My mother initiated me into it. As their link person to the outside world I have reached the pinnacle of marine cult. With that position I have the world in my pocket. I was very confidence with my spiritual powers not until Chiamaka came into this house.

[*She waves her head*]

I was meant to see marine powers as supreme. I am very sorry for many Christians all over the world because many of them are ignorant of the magnitude of the power vested on them. Many move about as Christians but are not a force to marine spirits. Chiamaka's presence in this house has caused a big crack in the marine kingdom of this territory. Anytime she prays from this house and mentions that name Jesus Christ there is always confusion in their kingdom. In the marine world we are not afraid of the kind of anointing a Christian has but the position of Christ in the life of that particular Christian. Oh my God will God ever forgive me of this?

[*She weeps*].

[*At this stage the bell rings revenue officers and some police officers come in*].

Chief Revenue Officer—Chief Udofia we have a court warrant to impound your properties for failing to pay your tax for the past ten years. You owe the federal government 30million naira

[*Outside the building already—the towing van is starting to tow his cars and a sign bearing for sale is placed on his house*].

SCENE 36

IN PRISON CELL

[*Kodo and Tony are seen in a serious discussion in Kodo's corner*].

Kodo—There is an order from a very high level for the inmates here to kill you. What exactly is your offence?

Tony—[*Very shocked and frightened. He opens his mouth to say something but could not*].

Kodo—You don't need to fear. The order was given to me to carry it out and save myself from death penalty but I will not do it.

Tony—[*Managed to say*]

But why?

Kodo—For the first time in my life my spirit is disturbed. I can't just say why. To kill is nothing new to me but this time and for the first time I even regret all my previous killings. Something is wrong with me. Don't you think so?

Tony—[*Raises his two hands up*]

I thank God for you. I believe the Holy Spirit wants to use you

Kodo—[*Opens his eyes wide*]

Holy what you mean I am possessed by a spirit? How does it operate? Does it kill? Please tell me because I can feel it all over my body and it is moving around. [*music—all over me*]

Tony—I believe God wants to make use of you to do something great.

Kodo—If I may ask are you a member of the Ultimate Club?

Tony—What does that mean?

Kodo—Ultimate Club is the highest and the most dangerous secret cult in this country but they operate as an ordinary social club. They are deadly. Who is the girl they say you kidnapped?

Tony—I don't even know much about her but she lives with Chief Udofia.

Kodo—No wonder now you are talking. Chief Udofia's wife is a member of that club. My brother you have really fallen into the hand of Satan himself. Now go to your corner let me confer with my men.

SCENE 37

POLICE STATION
Sgt. Bello is seen making entries. People are seen moving around within the station. Suddenly there comes an unusual noise of fighting and beating emanating from the detention room across.

Sgt. Bello—[*Very confused and picks the phone*]

Chief Sir there is a serious uprising going on in the cell what do I do sir?

Special Effect—Chief—[*Seen replying to the Sgt.*] All you need to do is leave them alone and mind your job make sure you don't go in there for any thing.

[*He drops the phone*]

As the Sgt. is about to drop the phone an inmate comes to the iron bars separating them from the outside.

Inmate—They have killed one prisoner.

Sgt. Bello—What?

[*These time the police Chief comes down the stairs*].

Police Chief—Any problem?

Sgt. Bello—[*Stood at attention*]

No problem sir except prisoners killed one prisoner

Police Chief—And you said no problem. Give me the files of the inmates accused of kidnapping.

[*Sgt. Bello brings two files and gives them, which he takes from him, writes something in them, and gives them back to him*]

You give the two files to the wife and tell her the husband was released yesterday.

Now listen to me if I leave here just tell any one who needs to know that they have been released. If any one asks of them their papers were signed two days ego. Make no mistakes about it. Let me have Kodo's file also.

. [*The file is given to him in it he does the same thing*].

The body of the dead prisoner should not be removed. I will do that myself.

When the Chief has gone Sgt. Bello takes the documents and starts to read. He looks shocked and confused. He picks up the phone and spoke—

Sgt. Bello—Please bring Mrs. Martins here.

[*He drops the phone and goes and opens the cell*]

Tony Martins and John Amadi come here.

[*Tony and Kodo come out*].

I am really confused—what is really going on here. The Chief has just signed your release papers. You are all free to go.

[*At this stage a policewoman leads Tony's wife in*].

[*The Sgt. hands them their papers one after the other*].

SCENE 38

PASTOR'S HOUSE

The Pastor watches a program in the TV when the bell rings, he gets up and opens the door for Chief Udofia.

Chief Udofia—How is my wife—I hope she is fine?

Pastor—Our Lord is still in control.

[*Indicating for him to sit down*]

Chief what is going on we are really worried about you.

Chief Udofia—I think the wrath of God is upon me. I am finished. Pastor I am finished.

Pastor—[*Takes a seat near to him*]

What happened?

Chief Udofia—All my investments have gone. Container goods worth over 30million seized, my accounts frozen, my estates including my personal houses to be sold.

The most painful part of it is that all my friends seem to avoid me as if I am carrying a contagious disease.

[*He weeps silently*]

What have I done to deserve this?

At this stage Akwaeke accompanied by the pastor's wife and Chiamaka come out to see him. Akwaeke opens her mouth and starts to sing—

> *Oh that day—I remember that day*
> *I can never forget that day when Jesus took my sins off me*
> *When Jesus took my sins off me*
> *Oh Calvary—I remember Calvary. I can never forget Calvary where Jesus died and set me free. Where Jesus died and set me free*
> *Oh Gethsemane—I remember Gethsemane I can never forget that garden where Jesus wept he wept for my sin.*
> *Where Jesus wept—He wept for my sins*

As she continues to make this confession in songs and in tears Chiamaka and the Pastor's wife are weeping also while chief is wiping his face with a white handkerchief.

After an interval she calms down and is led indoors by them.

Chief Udofia—*[When the wife has gone]*

Oh my God why have you pushed me into this marriage. I was rich before I married her. Now my business empire has collapsed. Oh my God I am finished. Every thing I labored for in life. How do I start again?

[He himself broke down the pastor left him to answer the doorbell].

Pastor—*[Shouts very loud]*

Tony! What happened?

[*Chiamaka and Pastor's wife run out with joy to welcome Tony and his wife*]

Tony—I give God the glory. He alone can explain what happened. All I know is that here are my papers in it they made it clear I was falsely accused and the papers were signed two days ego. The most disturbing aspect of the whole thing is that the Chief Thug in my cell was given the mandated by the police to kill me.

[*They all gasped in shock*]

[*At this stage Akwaeke comes in but this time she is not crying*].

Mrs. Udofia—Tony I am sorry for what happened to you and your wife. Your problem was conceived and executed in the marine spirit world. You could have prevented it if you had not allowed Chiamaka into your house just like my husband. I only thank God because I am free from marine bondage.

[*She goes and kneels down before her husband*]

Chief I am sorry for everything that has happened. I am totally responsible. Our marriage was initiated, planned and sealed in the marine spirit world it was the promise they made to me to give me a rich man as a husband. Please Chief forgive me.

[*Others joined to ask Chief to forgive*]

Chief Udofia—Well—I forgive.

SCENE 39

IN THE SPIRIT WORLD
The queen of the ocean addresses her special agents.

Queen—[*Looks very angry and terribly*]

Akwaeke's position as a link person to the outside world is broken and this might effect our operations very much.

[*She nods her head*]

She knows every secret behind our operations.

[*This time she spoke with anger*]

I will so deal with that family, I will reduce them to nothing. Udofia's family must beg bread in this country unless they repent and come back to me.

[*Seems to calm down*]

The purpose of our gathering now is to access the end time events. The entire prophecy prior to the coming of the righteous one for his people is systematically been fulfilled for example—

[*With special effect as the queen mentions them clips of such events taking place in the world will be shown*].

   [1] Mathew 24:11,24 Many false prophets shall come in my name.

[2] Mathew 24:6—7 wars and rumors of war and nations shall arise against nation. And there shall be famines, pestilence's, and earthquakes in diverse places

[3] Mathew 24:9 Persecution of Christians all over the world.

[4] Rev. 13:13 there shall be great signs and wonders to deceive many.

[5] Rev. 13:16—17 One world social, political, economic and religious system

[*The Queen looks at them with terror in her eyes*]

He will come as stated but will he find any one to follow him. Any one who is not with us is against us and should never be allowed to pollute others. I want every one of you to bear this in mind—God hates sin. The only way to separate mankind from God is to make them live in sin. Our main aim at this end time is to make it impossible for any person to make money without committing sin. Now I want that police chief who out of stupidity released those bastards from detention I want him now.

[*With special effect the police chief is seen at the reception reading from a document she points her fingers to him in the screen and it turns into blood*]

Bastard you must now go to hell.

SCENE 40

IN POLICE STATION
The Police Chief is barking like a dog to the police officer that replaced Sgt. Bello.

Police Chief—Where is Sgt. Bello? And where is the dead prisoner he told me of?

New Police Officer—Sgt. Bello is off duty today sir. No prisoner is dead sir.

Police Chief—What do you mean? Okay where are those prisoners accused of kidnapping.

New Police Officer—They have gone? These are their release papers signed by you sir

[*He quickly gets the papers from the drawers and gives them to him*].

Police Chief—[*Almost mad with him*]

Who told you to let them go? Are you mad? Let me see the papers.

[*He takes the papers from him by force and starts to read through, it is at this stage he starts to slump. The papers fall from his hand and scatter all over the floor. He tries to control himself but he can not. Before the new police officer could reach him he falls down with a great force. The new police officer runs to the phone and calls for help. Within a few minutes police ambulance arrives and he is taken to the hospital where doctors confirm him dead as a result of stroke.*

SCENE 41

IN CHIEF'S HOUSE

Chief is seen in his sitting room going through his documents and packing them into a brief case. The doorbell rings and he goes and opens the door only to be confronted by a very beautiful girl. Before Chief could say a word she was already inside his living room. Her dress was very provocative.

Emily—[*Smiling and acting in a very seductive manner*]

Chief I know you are very surprised to see me and I know you must have forgotten. I am Emily a public relation consultant. I read in the papers about your present ordeal. You may not remember I was the lady you gave a ride once when I was stranded at the airport

[*At this stage she turns and looks directly at his face with seducing smiles*]

I might be of good help to you in recovering your properties back. Remember one good turn deserves another. I have friends in the authority that might help.

Chief Udofia—You mean you can do that? Even this house is put for sale.

Emily—[*Displaying her under wears as she takes a sit*]

Lets me just see the documents.

Chief opened one of the brief cases and brought out files, which he gave to her.

The two sit together and start to go through the documents.

SCENE 42A

PASTOR'S HOUSE
The pastor is in the living room with his wife discussing matters.

Pastor's Wife—My dear if Chief does not come, what is going to be the fate of this woman and her children?

Pastor—May be he is looking for an alternative accommodation for them. Let us just wait and see.

Pastor's Wife—I am afraid that the Chief may not be able to come for them. My spirit keeps telling me that.

Pastor—Please reject that idea if he does that how can she manage in this place. I believe God he will come.

At this stage the bell rings and the pastor's wife goes and opens the door for Chika. She is in tears and behaving like some one being pursued or some one having a nightmare. The pastor and his wife are very confused and surprised.

SCENE 42B

PASTOR'S HOUSE—NEXT ROOM
Akwaeke and Chiamaka are in discussion.

Akwaeke—Chi I am not feeling fine. I feel very guilty concerning the whole thing. I will not be surprised if Chief abandons us here. That feeling is all over me. I know him very well. He loves money so much; he can do anything to recover his wealth back. I also know the activities of marine cult, these witches will never rest until they see a total destruction of my family and me.

[She turns and looks at Chiamaka]

Chi have you forgiven me? You see with you around me I feel more confident. I have the feeling Chief will never look for us again. He has not come for the past three days. I am going to make an alternative arrangement because I don't want us to be a burden to this good Pastor and his family. I just have enough that may last for sometime. Chiamaka will you stay with me.

Chiamaka—Of course I will where else will I go?

[At this stage they are now hearing Chika's voice in the living room saying]

> *Voice—Pastor please pray for me please I am under attack.*

Akwaeke—*[Beckoning to Chiamaka to listen]*

Be quiet that must be Chika I think they are up to something Come let us go and see.

[*They came and saw Chika lying on the floor weeping*].

Pastor—[*Picking her up to stand*]

My daughter what exactly is wrong with you?

Chika—[*She can not look at anyone's face she pretends to speak with difficulty*]

Pastor I can't sleep in my house. They want to kill me.

Pastor—[*This time he sits on the center table opposite Chika and looks at her directly in the face*].

Chika I don't want to know who or what is disturbing you all you need is to come to Jesus and be saved. If you accept Jesus as Lord and personal savior—the spirit of God then dwells in you and these evil forces chasing you will not be able to stand before you. You claim to be a Christian but I am telling you now without the prince of peace dwelling in you, you can never have peace. If the son sets you free you are free indeed. Finally Chika are you now ready to invite Jesus Christ into your life.

[*With special effect some of these marine spirits were shown urging her to leave immediately. This time Chika gets up and starts to shiver like one having cold*]

Chika—I am going. I can't stay any more.

[She starts to leave]

Pastor—I command you in Jesus name be still.

[Chika stops but with special effect these spirits are shown running for their lives]

You came in here with a problem and you must not go back with it.

Chiamaka—Chika all you need is to confess and make a new covenant with Christ. Your salvation lies in your hand.

Chika—*[Starts to weep]*

I will not confess anything.

Akwaeke—*[Pleading with her]*

Chika this is a big opportunity for you to come out from them. Where is your covenant material? This is the time to destroy it. Don't you want to be free?

[Chika is seen running from unseen attackers, which only her can see. At a stage she seems to be pointing at them one after the other. With special effect these spirits are seen trying to force her to leave the room]

Pastor—*[Starts to speak in tongues]*

[With special effect these spirits are again seen running for their lives immediately the pastor prays in tongues].

Chika—[*She starts to weep and talks at the same time*]

I was sent here to cause confusion at least to set the whole place on fire.

Akwaeke—[*Stands up and goes to her*]

Chika where is the covenant materials.

Chika—[*pointing at her waist*]

[*Mrs. Udofia bends down and put her hand under her and breaks the covenant beads scattering them all over the places.*

SCENE 43

UDOFIA'S HOUSE

Emily is seen lying on the bed while Chief is seen standing in front of the mirror-adjusting his tie.

Emily—Chief where are you going? Are you going to see your wife?

[*She gets up from the bed bringing Chief down to the bed, kissing his face and neck*]

Chief I want to know what you feel about me I have spent the last three days with you and you've not even told me how you feel about me. At least we are able to recover your properties.

Chief Udofia—[*Kissing her back*]

I really have to be very frank with you the past three days we have been together seems to have taken away my burden. My stay with Akwaeke is always one day one trouble. That woman is a big witch. In short I must divorce her.

[At this stage the doorbell rings and Chief goes out only to open the door for his wife and Chiamaka]

Akwaeke—What is wrong?

Chief Udofia—*[Very shocked and surprised]*

With what?

Akwaeke—For the past three days you've not called or visited us. Have you made an alternative accommodation for us have they holed you up with a marine spirit?

[She starts to move into the house but Chief blocks her]

Chief I am afraid something is wrong with you.

Chief—*[Still blocking her]*

Where are you going? I have been trying to clear the backlog of problem you brought into this house with your witchcraft activities. You've almost ruined my life. Please the best thing for you to do now is to stay clear. I really want to arrange things the way they should be. Since you left I have been busy—I have almost recovered all the properties seized by the authority.

Akwaeke—*[Standing boldly before him]*

Chief who is the girl with you? For I know you have not been alone for the past three days.

Chief Udofia—How do you know? Who told you that?

Akwaeke—You are heading to a more terrible disaster.

Chief Udofia—[*Anger written all over his face*]

Now you can get out I have a lot to do.

Chiamaka—Chief please.

Chief Udofia—[*Seems to notice her for the first time*]

It is okay! That reminds me you must prepare to go home because since you stepped into this house we've been from one problem to another.

[*Pointing at his wife*]

If you have anything in this house take them now.

[*At this stage Emily is seen watching the whole scene from the pinhole she seems to be happy*].

Akwaeke—[*Kneeling down before him*]

Chief please for your life's sake and that of your children don't do that. Nothing good will ever come out of that road you are heading to.

Chief Udofia—I am only giving you 20minutes to take all that belong to you or I throw you out.

Akwaeke—[*Looks at him for a very long time*]

Chief my dear I hope you are with your senses. I am not afraid of facing divorce. I am only concerned with your soul. I have served Satan throughout my life I know how destructive he can be.

[*Still looking at him*]

Today I know Jesus Christ has given me peace of mind. Yes I am going now to collect my things but you will live to regret this

[*She beckons to Chiamaka as she moves into the bedroom. This time Emily sees them coming and runs to the bed and covers herself. Mrs. Udofia comes into the bedroom and starts to collect clothes from the wardrobe while Chiamaka packs them into a bag. This time Chief comes in and watches them. At a time Mrs. Udofia stops and looks at Emily who pretends to be sleeping.*]

Akwaeke—I want to make it clear to you that what you are seeing on this bed is not a human being they have sent her to destroy you finally.

Chief Udofia—Just pack your things and leave me alone. I can take care of myself.

Akwaeke—I have tested the two powers and I believe that Jesus Christ is the Lord of Lords.

[*At the mention of that name Emily shouts in a very strange voice*]

Emily—[*In a male's voice*]

Who mentioned that name here?

[*This time she starts to gyrate like a serpent, from the bed she falls to the floor and goes under the bed. From under the bed where she went comes another animalistic noise follows by smoke that fills the whole room. Mrs. Udofia and Chiamaka run out of the room. After a brief period when everything seems to have calmed down they came back and found Chief lying unconscious on the floor but Emily is no where to be found.*]

SCENE 44

IN THE SPIRIT WORLD

The Queen is with her special agents.

Queen—[*Looks very angry*]

Ogemma I sent you on a mission you spent the whole period having fun forgetting your aim which is to destroy the family.

Ogemma—[*Shaking all over*]

Oh my Queen the heat that stroke me when that name was mentioned was unbearably. I had no alternative but to run.

Queen—Shut up

[*Pointing her deadly finger on her*]

Now you must go to hell and continue your fun.

[*She is engulfed by smoke and starts to melt like wasp*]

[*She now turns and starts to address her agents*]

There is no other power greater than the one we possess here and in this kingdom there is no justification for failure.

[*She starts to call them one after the other*]

Agent for finance—

One agent stands up]

> [1] I want 70% of all the financial institutions in this country distressed.
> [2] Use every means within your power to reduce money in circulation.
> [3] Promote advanced free fraud to discredit the nation internationally.

Agent for Bureaucracy—

[*Another agent stands*]

> [1] I want you to destroy all values in the civil service
> [2] Encourage our human agents in government to siphon government fund.

[3] You must do every thing within your power to weaken the economic structure.

Now you spirit responsible for evangelism give me your report.

Spirit of Evangelism stands up

[1] Due to the world wide economic slump, the minds of the people is centered more on prosperity. We have been able to shift their minds from the righteous one to acquisition of wealth.
[2] Using the word of God found in—

Voice 2nd Corinthians 6:14—Be yea not unequally yoked together with unbelievers: for what fellowship hath righteousness with unrighteousness? And what communion hath light with darkness?

[2] We have been able to use this passage to encourage fornication and adultery within church members and many have been denied marriage based on this passage. In many churches and fellowship groups any marriage that is not contracted between members of the same church or fellowship group is unbiblical.
[3] Using the same Passage many have isolated themselves from their parents, communities, and even their churches therefore we have been able to plant discord amongst them.
[4] We have also planted many churches with our agents as leaders and they are performing great signs and wonders.

Queen—[*Nodding her head for approval*]

Thank you agent for evangelism you are doing fine. You are free to supply our men and women of God with all they need to carryout their duties.

Now I want the spirit of Chief Udofia on the screen.

[*The screen shows Chief on the hospital bed with pastor and others praying for him*].

Stop—I say stop.

[*This time the screen becomes blank*]

I want a full report on the doctor who owns that hospital immediately.

Computer Agent—

[1] The doctor belongs to Ultimate Club right from the university.
[2] He was the doctor who performed the ultimate assignment on Chiamaka's mother when he was on national service in their village.

Queen—I see—I must see him myself.

SCENE 45

IN THE HOSPITAL

Chief lays on the bed, his wife sits at his bedside weeping silently while the doctor is seen doing some examination on him. Outside his room the pastor, Chiamaka; and pastor's wife are seen waiting. At the hospital reception a beautiful lady is seen talking to the receptionist. She leaves the receptionist and beckons to a nurse who seems to recognize her.

Lady Ann—Call the doctor and tell him I want to see him I am waiting for him in his office.

The nurse goes straight into Chief's room and whispers something to the doctor who stops everything he is doing and left. Mrs. Udofia seems confused and surprised.

As the doctor comes out the pastor stops him.

Pastor—How is he doing Doc.?

Doctor—He is doing fine.

Pastor—May we then continue our prayer?

Doctor—No problem—you may continue.

[He leaves them]

Inside the doctor's office Lady Ann sits on the visitor's seat while the doctor stands in her presence visibly shaken.

Lady Ann—*[Pointing at the doctor's seat]*

Sit down doc. I am very impressed with your record of service to our great club the Ultimate Club. Just keep it up. We have recommended you for the post of minister of health it will be confirmed in the next Cabinet meeting. Now I have a job for you I want the blood of Chief Udofia tonight in our blood bank.

This assignment really shocked him. He just looks at her and seems not to be seeing her. This time his mind went straight to the last job he did for the Lady.

FLASH BACK

SCENE 46

HOSPITAL LABOR ROOM

Mrs. Uche Okafor has just successfully delivered her baby and lays unconscious while the baby lay by her side. This time the doctor comes in and asks the entire nurses to leave with the exception of Joy. She looks at him.

Doctor—Ultimate Assignment.

[*The nurse nods her head and brings the instrument for blood transfusion. At this stage Mrs. Okafor wakes up.*

Mrs. Uche Okafor—How is my baby?

Nurse Joy—She is fine—just relax madam.

[*She then puts the syringe into her vein and starts to collect her blood into a blood bag. This time Mrs. Uche has gone into a very dip sleep. After this the nurse hands over the blood bag to the doctor who takes it and goes straight to the doctor's dressing room where Lady Ann was seen waiting.*

SCENE 47

STILL IN THE DOCTOR'S OFFICE

Lady Ann is visibly shaken like a leaf. With special effect she is able to hear a noise that shakes the whole place.

Lady Ann—[*Looks very frightened and her voice brings the doctor back to reality*]

Do you organize crusade in this hospital?

Doctor—[*Just back from his dream*]

A pastor and members of Udofia's family are praying for him.

Lady Ann—[*Full of anger*] Go and send them away.

[*She gets up and before the doctor can say anything she is already on the door*].

I want this item by tomorrow's night and make no mistakes about it.

[*With that statement she just melts away*]

[*Immediately when she leaves the doctor presses the intercom and nurse Joy comes in*]

Doctor—[*They just look at each other for a long time*]

Please sit down.

Nurse Joy—Why is she here?

Doctor—Ultimate assignment on Chief Udofia.

Nurse Joy—[*Shouts in shock*]

What! Why?

Doctor—Will you go and ask her?

Nurse Joy—Is the wife no more serving her?

Doctor—She seems to be a born again. Now go and clear that room. Tell every person to leave including his wife we are to perform a minor operation on him tonight.

Don't give them any clue to be suspicious. Chief is an important person in this country.

Nurse Joy—[*She gets up*]

Doctor this is a very delicate assignment you should have told her that.

Doctor—Are you off your senses? To argue with that witch, Please go and do what you are told.

[*She closes the door and left*]

SCENE 48

IN HOSPITAL ROOM
The Pastor is just concluding the prayer when Nurse Joy comes in.

Nurse Joy—The doctor wants every body out he wants to perform a minor operation on him.

[*Mrs. Udofia is visibly shaken and confused as they all come out. This time the doctor has arrived.*

Doctor—I will perform a minor operation on him tonight and the operation may last 2 hours. After that he will have two days rest. It is better you leave him alone now for he needs to rest and prepare for it.

[*He forces a smile and leaves them*]

SCENE 49

STILL IN THE HOSPITAL
Akwaeke—[*Weeping*]

Pastor I am afraid something is wrong somewhere but I can't figure it out. The reaction of the doctor when that nurse whispered something to him is still bordering me. The whole drama to me is suspicious. Now they are talking of operation.

Pastor—Be still for our God is in control.

[*At this stage Chika is seen coming towards them and she seems to be in a hurry*].

Chika—[*Runs straight to Akwaeke*]

Did you see Lady Ann?

[*Before she could complete the statement Akwaeke shouts at top of her voice*]

Akwaeke—Lady What? Oh my God they want the blood of my husband. Never!

[*She runs into the room and removes the transfusion instrument from Chief's hand while the doctor and Nurse Joy stand helplessly. This time pastor and the rest come and help her to carry him out of the room. Akwaeke runs back and collects the instrument and goes away with it.*

SCENE 50

IN THE SPIRIT WORLD
The Queen addresses members of her special agents.

Queen—Anytime from now Ultimate Club will take over the government. When that happens the present economic problem will be a child's play to compare with the one to come. Reports reaching us from other countries show that plans to dismantle all existing national governments have reached an advanced stage and any time from now the one world government will take off. Now I want that stupid doctor who failed the ultimate assignment.

[*With special effect the doctor is seen on the screen. She just points her finger on the screen and it becomes bloody*]

SCENE 51

DOCTOR'S OFFICE
The doctor and the nurse are sitting opposite each other ,they seem to be in a state of panic.

Doctor—[*Visibly shaking and looking at nurse*]

I am taking my sabbatical leave. You take care of everything till I come back. Is there any reaction from Chief Udofia's family?

Nurse Joy—None so far.

Doctor—Any news from that witch? She must have known that the assignment has failed. I am leaving, that woman is a cannibal.

[*He gets up to leave but can not because of pain in his chest. At this stage he starts to slump and falls heavily on the floor. Joy runs out and calls other nurses who help to carry him into the operating room. He is later confirmed dead.*]

SCENE 52

CHIEF UDOFIA'S HOUSE
Chief is seen been led from a car into his sitting room by his wife and the others. He sits down and seems to have recovered, his wife cleans his face.

Pastor—*[Addressing Chief]*

Chief to avoid a future manipulation by the devil and his agents you need to invite Jesus Christ into your life and start up a closer relationship with him.

Chief—*[Looking confused]*

I have never belonged to any cult or secret society. I do my best to help those who are less privilege.

Pastor—I will read a portion of the bible to you—

> *Voice*—*If we say that we have no sin, we deceive ourselves, and the truth is not in us. If we confess our sins, he is faithful and just to forgive us our sins, and cleans us from all unrighteousness. If we say that we have not sinned we make him a liar and his word is not in us.*

[Closing the book]

Chief I want you to understand this fact. God created the world but the system that governs the world today was introduced by Satan. The sin of Adam separated us from God's control and brought in the present world system. The bible calls Satan the prince of this world. Before the fall of the human race through the sin of Adam God gave man control over all the things he created now listen to this

> *Voice Genesis 1:27—28 So God created man in his own image, in the image of God created he him; male and female created he them. And God blessed them, and God*

> *said unto them, Be fruitful, and multiply, and replenish*
> *the earth, and subdue It: and have dominion over the*
> *fish of the sea, and the fowl of the air, and over every*
> *living thing that moveth upon the earth.*

The sin of Adam deprived the human race of this wonderful opportunity and opened the door for the present world order. In spiritual politics there is no neutral party.

If you have not given Jesus Christ the authority to control and direct your life the devil will always be in control. There is no two ways about it.

That is why anytime the devil wants you to commit sin you just do it without any feeling of regret. In this case it is only your mind can define what is sin to you. Chief I am not talking religion. You may be a Christian, Hindus, Buddhist, Muslim or even a pagan. Believe it or not the greatest sin today in a man's life is when he rejects the gift of God which is eternal life.

The bible says in—

> *Voice—Romans 6:23 For the wages of sin is death; but*
> *the gift of God is eternal life through Jesus Christ our*
> *Lord.*

Jesus Christ is a special gift from God to redeem mankind from the penalty of sin, which is hell fire. Now look at your wife when Jesus Christ took over all those demons that controlled her life for the past years left and today she is free the same with Chika.

Without Christ you can do nothing this might be the only chance you have. The choice is yours. Are you now willing to give him a chance to take control?

[*This time Chief looks at him and nods in agreement he then kneels down in total surrender*] *THE MUSIC—I SURRENDER ALL*

THE END

WRITTEN BY BROTHER
JONATHAN EZEMEKA
ENUGU NIGERIA
Dedicated to all believers worldwide